Collins · *do brilliantly !*   Viv Bound

■ **Claire Meldrum**

InstantRevision

■ Series Editor:
Jayne de Courcy

ASPsychology

Contents

Published by HarperCollins*Publishers* Ltd
77-85 Fulham Palace Road
London W6 8JB

www.**Collins**Education.com
On-line support for schools and colleges

First published 2002
This new format edition published 2004
10 9 8 7 6 5 4 3 2 1

ISBN 0 00 717271 0

British Library Cataloguing in Publication Data
A catalogue record for this book is available from the British Library.

Edited by Brigitte Lee
Production by Katie Butler
Design by Gecko Ltd
Illustrations by Gecko Ltd
Printed and bound by Printing Express Ltd, Hong Kong

You might also like to visit:
www.**fire**and**water**.com
The book lover's website

Get the most out of your Instant Revision pocket book

1 **Maximise your revision time.** You can carry this book around with you anywhere. This means you can spend any spare moments revising.

2 **Learn and remember what you need to know.** The book contains all the really important facts you need to know for your exam. All the information is set out clearly and concisely, making it easy for you to revise.

3 **Find out what you don't know.** The *Check yourself* questions help you to discover quickly and easily the topics you're good at and those you're not so good at.

What's in this book

1 What you need to know for AS Psychology

- This book covers all the **five core areas** for AS Psychology Specification A set by the AQA exam board:
  - Cognitive Psychology (Human memory)
  - Developmental Psychology (Attachments in development)
  - Physiological Psychology (Stress)
  - Individual Differences (Abnormality)
  - Social Psychology (Social influence)
  plus Research methods.

- Each core area, plus Research methods, is divided into three topics (which includes a critical issue in each area, except for Research methods). **Each chapter in this book deals with one of the specified 18 topics** (see Contents on page i).

- All topics specified by AQA are compulsory. Although there is some choice of questions in the exam, there will not necessarily be a question on everything that is shown on the specification. **It is therefore important that you revise all topics.**

2 Help with developing the skills assessed in AS Psychology

- In your exam you will be assessed on your **knowledge and understanding** ('Assessment Objective 1': AO1) and on your **skills of analysis and evaluation** ('Assessment Objective 2': AO2). In the Research methods area you are assessed on your **ability to design, conduct and report** ('Assessment Objective 3': AO3).

- The answers are given at the back of the book. When you have answered the questions, check your answers with those given.

3 *Check yourself* questions – find out how much you know and improve your grade

- The *Check yourself* questions appear at the end of each short topic. They are not actual exam questions. However, they provide a test of the kind of knowledge you are required to demonstrate (AO1 skill) and comment on (AO2 skill) in the exam.

- When you have answered the questions, check your answers with those given at the back of the book.

- There are marks for each question. If you score very low marks for a particular *Check yourself* page, this shows that you are weak on that topic and need to put in more revision time.

●Revise actively!

- **Concentrated, active revision** is much more successful than spending long periods reading through notes with half your mind on something else.

- For each of your revision sessions, choose a couple of topics and concentrate on reading and thinking them through for **20–30 minutes**. Then do the *Check yourself* questions. If you get a number of questions wrong, you will need to return to the topic at a later date.

Memory is the storing of information over time. It consists of three processes: Encoding - placing information into memory.

Storage - retaining information in memory.

Retrieval - recovering information from memory.

There are different **types** of memory, including:

● **Sensory memory** (SM) - for storing an exact copy of sensory stimuli for a fraction of a second

● **Short-term memory** (STM) - for storing information for brief periods of time

● **Long-term memory** (LTM) - for storing information for long periods of time

Sensory memory (SM)

● This is where sensory data are held until a decision is made as to whether further processing is required. We probably have a SM for each of our senses, e.g. iconic memory for visual stimuli and echoic memory for auditory stimuli. A selective attention process allows only limited information to pass from SM to STM for further processing.

Short-term memory (STM)

● STM has a limited **capacity**, measured by looking at STM span. For example, participants listen to a list of random digits and immediately afterwards they try to recollect them in the correct order. Miller (1956) found that most adults recalled seven plus or minus two bits (or 'chunks') of information (called the 'magic number seven'). A 'chunk' is a unit of information, e.g. a letter or number or word. Other researchers have found that people remember more short words than long words in tests of STM capacity. They have concluded that **people can remember as many words as they can pronounce in 1.5 seconds.**

● Brown (1958) and Peterson and Peterson (1959) investigated the **duration** of STM by showing participants a consonant trigram (e.g. BVT) and asking them to recall it after delays ranging from 3 to 18 seconds. Participants carried out an interference task (e.g. counting backwards in threes) to prevent them rehearsing the trigram before recalling it. About 80% of trigrams were recalled correctly after 3 seconds but only 10% after 18 seconds. They concluded that **information is lost from STM after only a few seconds unless it is rehearsed**

● When information enters memory it is **encoded** (coded for storage) in a number of different ways. For example, the word 'coat' may be coded acoustically (the sound of the word) or visually (the image of a coat) or semantically (the meaning of the word 'coat' and, e.g., when one might wear it). **Acoustic coding is preferred in STM** and Baddeley (1966) found that lists of words that sound similar (e.g. mad, map etc.) are harder to remember than lists of words that sound dissimilar (e.g. big, large etc.) even though they have similar meanings.

Long-term memory (LTM)

● Unlike STM, LTM seems to have **unlimited storage capacity**.

● It is difficult to establish the **duration** of LTM, but research shows that some memories last a lifetime. For example, Bahrick et al. (1975) found that American ex-high school students could still name 90% of their old classmates when shown their photographs, even though some participants had left high school 34 years earlier.

● **Semantic encoding** is important in LTM. The more meaningful information is, the better it is stored in LTM. Baddeley found that similarity of meaning caused confusion when participants tried to recall words from LTM but that acoustic similarity of words did not interfere with their recall from LTM (though you will remember that this did impair recall from STM).

● **Visual and acoustic coding** also occur in LTM (e.g. picturing a scene from a favourite film or remembering a popular tune), and tastes and smells are also stored. Therefore LTM is flexible, long-lasting and apparently has unlimited capacity.

Models of memory

Models of memory attempt to explain either **how** information passes from STM to LTM or **why** it is that some information is retained for only a short time while other information is remembered for a lifetime.

The multi-store model of memory (Atkinson and Shiffrin 1968)

● Information passes from one storage system to the next in a **fixed order**.

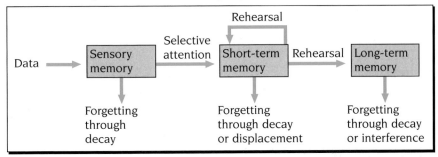

● SM, STM and LTM are seen as **permanent structures** of the memory system.

● The process of **selective attention** allows only specific information to enter conscious STM.

● **Rehearsal** (repeating information verbally) is another control process that permits information to be maintained in STM or to be transferred to LTM.

Evaluation of the multi-store model

● **Case studies** of people with brain damage have provided some evidence in support of this model. In some cases STM is impaired but LTM remains intact, suggesting that there are two separate stores involved. However, we need to be cautious when generalizing findings from studies of brain-damaged people in an attempt to understand how memory works in the 'normal' population.

● **Laboratory studies** have shown the importance of rehearsal in enabling information to be passed from STM to LTM. For example,

Murdock (1962) asked participants to memorise a list of words and then free-recall as many as they could immediately afterwards. Both **primacy** and **recency effects** were observed. That is, the first and last words in the list were recalled best. It is assumed that the words first in the list had been rehearsed and passed into LTM, whereas the words last in the list were still accessible from STM. When Glanzer and Cunitz (1966) delayed recall for 30 seconds but prevented participants rehearsing the words during this time by using an **interference task**, the primacy effect was maintained but the recency effect disappeared. Those words at the end of the list were prevented from transferring from STM into LTM.

● The multi-store model is criticised for **oversimplifying the memory process**.
  ■ Baddeley and Hitch's (1974) working memory model (see below) challenges the idea of a unitary short-term store.
  ■ Research on explicit (conscious) and implicit (unconscious) memory challenges the idea of a unitary LTM.
  ■ There is also evidence of incidental (unintentional) learning where information is not rehearsed but nevertheless enters LTM.

The working memory model

Baddeley and Hitch (1974) challenged the concept of a unitary STM store and proposed instead a multi-component working memory (WM), comprising a central control mechanism and a number of slave (or sub-) systems. A simplified version of the WM model is shown in the diagram:

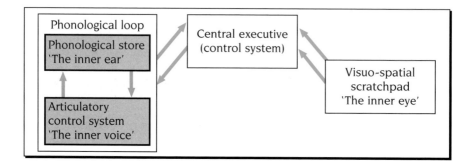

- The central executive has a limited capacity but is flexible and involved in processes such as attending, problem-solving and decision-making.

- The visuo-spatial scratchpad (or sketchpad) has a limited capacity and is used to store visually coded information such as size, colour and spatial relationships. It is known as the 'inner eye'.

- The phonological loop has a time-based capacity of about 2 seconds. It consists of two parts: (a) the phonological store (or 'inner ear') stores acoustically coded items for short periods, and (b) the articulatory control system (or 'inner voice') is linked to speech production and also enables us to rehearse information subvocally, which is particularly useful when we have to read difficult material.

Evaluation of the working memory model

- The chief weakness is that little is known about the capacity or precise functioning of the central executive.

- However, the WM model explains how we are able to store information briefly while actively processing it at the same time in such tasks as mental arithmetic and verbal reasoning.

- Research evidence (e.g. Baddeley and Hitch 1976) supports the existence of limited capacity, independent slave systems.

- It is still not clear what happens to information that is not coded in either the phonological loop or the visuo-spatial scratchpad, e.g. memory for touch or smell.

The levels of processing theory (LOP)

- Craik and Lockhart (1972) rejected Atkinson and Shiffrin's notion of separate memory structures (see the multi-store model) and instead proposed that it is how deeply information is analysed or processed that determines how well it is remembered. In other words, deep processing leads to more elaborate and longer-lasting memory traces than shallow processing.

● Craik and Lockhart (1973, p. 48) defined **depth as 'the meaningfulness extracted from the stimulus'**. Semantic analysis, therefore, is an example of deep processing, whereas physical analysis (e.g. noting whether a word is written in lower or upper case) is an example of shallow processing. Rote repetition, without any elaboration, is another example of shallow processing.

Evaluation of levels of processing theory

● It has been suggested that the reason semantic processing results in better retention is simply because **analysing material for meaning takes longer** rather than because it is 'deeper'. However, Craik and Tulving's (1975) experiment where shallow processing was designed to take longer than semantic processing still resulted in better retention following semantic ('deep') processing.

● The main criticism of LOP relates to **the circularity of its argument**. There is no definition of 'depth of processing' that is independent of how well material is remembered. The reasoning goes thus: How do we know material has been deeply processed? Because it has been memorised. Why has material been memorised? Because it has been deeply processed.

● Other researchers have claimed that it is processing **effort** (rather than depth) that aids memory and Craik and Lockhart (1986) have also pointed out the importance of **elaborating** material and making it **distinctive** as important for improving retention.

Short-term and long-term memory

1 Name the **three** processes involved in memory. (3)

2 How many chunks of information can be held in STM? (1)

3 In STM which type of coding is preferred? (1)

4 Give the procedure and findings from Bahrick et al.'s study, using ex-high school students, to find out whether memories could last a lifetime. (2)

5 What is semantic encoding? (1)

6 Give **three** key features of the multi-store model of memory. (3)

7 Name **two** areas of research that have provided evidence in support of the multi-store model. (2)

8 Name the **three** components of the working memory model. (3)

9 In what way does **one** of the working memory subsystems help us understand difficult written material? (1)

10 What is the main weakness of the working memory model? (1)

11 Briefly outline the levels of processing theory of memory. (1)

12 Give the main criticism made of the levels of processing theory. (1)

Exam tip

In your AS Psychology course, certain areas are identified where you are required to have detailed knowledge of one research study. You need to know about the aims, procedures, findings, conclusions and criticisms of one study in each 'key' area. For example, you might be asked to 'Describe the procedures and findings of **one** study of duration of STM'. Take care to **provide only the information asked for**. In this case, you would earn no marks if you also wrote about aims or conclusions or criticisms.

The answers are on page 109.

Forgetting occurs either because:

- A memory is unavailable (has ceased to exist), or because
- A memory is inaccessible (cannot be located but still exists).

There are several theories that try to explain why forgetting happens. Some theories are concerned with when memories become unavailable and others are concerned with why memories become inaccessible.

Forgetting in short-term memory (STM)

Forgetting in STM occurs when memories become unavailable. Exactly how forgetting happens is unclear, but the processes of displacement, decay and interference probably play a part.

Displacement theory

- Old information is replaced by newer information.
- Research using the serial probe technique offers some support for this theory. For example, a participant is presented with a set of 16 digits. One digit (the probe) is repeated and the participant tries to recall the digit that followed it. Recall is significantly better if the probe is from near the end of the list than from near the start (Norman 1965).

Decay theory

- Information is forgotten when its physical 'trace' fades and eventually disappears owing to the passage of time and lack of rehearsal.
- A study by Peterson and Peterson (see pp.1–2) showed that recall was worse after 18 seconds than after 3 seconds. This appears to support the decay theory. However, the poorer recall after 18 seconds could have been caused by interference from the counting task (actually called an interference task) that was used to prevent rehearsal.

Interference theory

- Forgetting occurs when other information gets in the way of what needs to be remembered.

- Research shows that interference from similar material causes more forgetting than interference from dissimilar material.

Forgetting in long-term memory (LTM)

Many theories have been proposed to explain why forgetting happens in LTM. These include the following:

Decay theory

- If skills are not practised or material is not rehearsed then their physical traces will disappear eventually.

- This is a difficult theory to test and evidence exists to show that some skills (e.g. bike riding) and some information not used for many years are nevertheless not forgotten. The mere passage of time might play a part in forgetting but other factors are more important.

Interference theory

- Two types of interference have been described:
  - Proactive interference (PI): when old information interferes with remembering new information.
  - Retroactive interference (RI): when new information interferes with retrieving old memories.

- Several experiments have demonstrated PI and RI. However, most studies of interference have been conducted in laboratory settings and therefore are far removed from the real-life situations where forgetting causes problems.

- Tulving (1966) also showed that interference is not a fully adequate explanation of forgetting. Previously learned information that is not recalled at one trial may be recalled at a later trial. In other words, the material was available but not always accessible. Forgetting, therefore, may happen because of difficulties at the time of retrieving the memories.

Retrieval failure

● Retrieval failure refers to the inability to access a memory even though the memory is available. This occurs when there are inadequate cues to prompt remembering.

● Tulving and Psotka's (1971) research demonstrated that much forgetting when free recall was used was cue dependent (caused by a lack of appropriate cues) rather than the result of RI.

● Memories are best retrieved when cues are:
  ■ encoded at the same time as the memory (e.g. a category heading given with a number of examples), or
  ■ similar to the memories being sought (e.g. if you are trying to recall a name and someone suggests a similar name).

Role of context

● Forgetting may be reduced if attempts at remembering take place in a similar context to that in which the original memorising was done.

● Godden and Baddeley (1975) studied memory in deep-sea divers. They found that divers forgot most material (list of words) if they learned and then recalled it in different situations (above or below water). The environmental context presumably acted as a retrieval cue to improve recall for those who learned and recalled the words in the same situation.

Role of emotion

● Internal psychological states can act as retrieval cues, rather as external contexts do. Memories encoded while one is happy are best retrieved when one is again in a happy mood.

● Ucros (1989) found that mood dependence is more pronounced in adults than in children, more obvious in real-life than laboratory situations and stronger when moods are positive than negative.

Repression

● According to Freud, some memories cannot be easily accessed because they have been **repressed**, i.e. forced from conscious awareness because they provoke too much anxiety.

● This theory is **difficult to test for ethical and practical reasons**. However, there is interest in memories of child abuse 'recovered' during psychotherapy. Some adults seem to have repressed their memories of being abused. Sometimes, however, there is no corroborative evidence to confirm these 'recovered' memories. Furthermore, Loftus (1997) has shown that memories can be altered by means of suggestion and post-event questioning (see next chapter).

Flashbulb memories

● Brown and Kulik (1977) coined the term **flashbulb memory** to describe a type of memory where emotion acts to improve recollection. Flashbulb memories are defined as **vivid, detailed, long-lasting and usually relating to highly significant, emotional and often unexpected events** (e.g. the death of Princess Diana).

● Neisser (1982), however, does not accept that flashbulb memories are fundamentally different from other memories. He claims that such memories persist because they are frequently recounted but are liable to the same types of inaccuracy and forgetting as other memories.

● Conway et al. (1994), on the other hand, disagree. Their research found that when an event (such as Mrs Thatcher's resignation in 1990) was **truly surprising** and **significant** (had consequences for people's lives) it led to consistent, detailed and enduring memories. 86% of the UK sample still had flashbulb memories after 11 months compared to only 29% of participants from other countries. In Brown and Kulik's study 75% of black participants reported flashbulb memories for the death of Martin Luther King compared to only 33% of white participants.

Check yourself

Forgetting

1 Is it lack of availability or lack of accessibility that causes forgetting in STM? (1)

2 Outline the decay theory of forgetting in STM. (2)

3 What experimental technique has been used to demonstrate displacement as a cause of forgetting in STM? (1)

4 Explain retroactive interference and proactive interference. (2)

5 What is cue-dependent forgetting in LTM? (1)

6 What two features of a cue enhance its ability to aid memory? (2)

7 Why is it a good idea to practise/learn material for an examination in conditions as like those of the real exam as possible? (1)

8 What name did Freud give the process where anxiety-provoking memories are forced out of conscious awareness? (1)

9 Why is it sometimes difficult to find out if memories 'recovered' during psychotherapy are true? (1)

10 List the features of a flashbulb memory according to Brown and Kulik (1977). (6)

11 Who challenged the concept of flashbulb memories as special, and why? (2)

Exam tip

Some questions will ask you to 'outline' something (e.g. 'outline Bowlby's maternal deprivation theory') for 6 marks. An outline is a pared down description and should be about 100–120 words long for a 6-mark question. Practise the skill of 'outlining'. It is harder than you think!

The answers are on pages 109–10.

The study of **eyewitness testimony (EWT)** is concerned with how accurately people can remember significant events (such as crimes) which they have witnessed. The consequences of inaccurate EWT may be serious especially as jurors are reported to be highly influenced by such evidence (Wells et al. 1979). Therefore, it is not surprising that psychologists should be interested in trying to find out what causes unreliable testimony and how to improve it. A number of different avenues of research have been pursued. These include the **reconstructive** nature of memory, the role of **leading questions**, and the **effects of fear and anxiety**.

Reconstructive memory

- Bartlett (1932) has demonstrated how **memory involves an active interpretation and reconstruction of events, influenced by our previous understanding and knowledge about similar events (our schemas).**

- English participants read an unfamiliar North American folk story 'The War of the Ghosts'. When the story was repeatedly retold (using the method of serial reproduction), Bartlett found that it underwent some marked changes; it became shorter, and more coherent and conventional from an English point of view. That is, the story was interpreted and reconstructed to fit the schema that the English participants held about story telling.

- **Schemas (schemata) are organised packages of knowledge about objects, events etc.,** built up through experience and stored in long-term memory. They provide frameworks to help us deal with new information and experiences. When schemas relate to social behaviours they are called **scripts** and consist of the stereotypical sequences of actions that are typical for a given occasion (such as visiting a restaurant).

- Schemas, which include stereotypes, are **important at the initial storage stage as well as at the retrieval stage of memory.** For example, Bransford and Johnson (1972 and 1973) showed that context-schemas helped participants understand and recall prose passages that were difficult to comprehend without such a context.

- **Schemas can affect memory** in a number of different ways (Cohen 1993):
  - We tend to **ignore information** that is incompatible with our existing schemas.
  - We **remember the gist of events** but not necessarily the details.
  - We use schema-based knowledge to **interpret** current situations and to **fill in gaps** in our memory.
  - **Memories may be distorted** so that events map on to existing schemas, e.g. if we have a stereotype that robbers wear masks we may, as witnesses, report seeing a mask worn when, in fact, the robber wore dark glasses or goggles (Willson 2000).
  - We use schemas to help us **guess** what probably happened when we cannot really remember.

Evaluation of reconstructive theory of memory

- It has proven **difficult to replicate** Bartlett's findings in more naturalistic settings. When Wynn and Logie (1998) tested students' memories for 'real-life' events during their first week at university they found high levels of accuracy and little use of reconstructive processes.

- There is some criticism about the failure to explain exactly **how schemas are acquired** in the first place.

- There is seldom any direct **evidence that participants actually possess the schemas** assumed to lead to their inaccurate memories.

- Schema theory is criticised for **implying that memory is usually inaccurate**, whereas many events and much information are remembered accurately.

Leading questions: research by Loftus

- **Language used to question witnesses can alter what they remember**. It is argued that information given after the event (in the form of how questions are worded) may actually change the memory stored for the event.

- Loftus and Palmer (1974) showed a film of a car accident. Some participants were asked how fast the cars were going when they 'hit' each other. Others were asked the same question but the word 'hit' was replaced with various other words, including 'smashed'. It was found that the **word used in the question affected the estimated speed**: 40mph for the 'smashed' condition and 34mph for the 'hit' condition. One week later, all the participants were asked if they had seen any broken glass. Although there had been no broken glass, 32% of those in the 'smashed' conditioned reported seeing it compared with only 14% of those in the 'hit' condition.

- **Even tiny changes in the language used in questioning may affect what witnesses recall**. Loftus and Zanni (1975) showed a short film of a car accident. Some eyewitnesses were asked if they had seen '**the**' broken headlamp, others if they had seen '**a**' broken headlamp. 17% of those asked about 'the' broken headlamp reported seeing it compared with only 7% of those who were asked about 'a' broken headlamp.

- However, Loftus has also shown that witnesses are not misled if the post-event misinformation is too blatantly incorrect.

- Misleading post-event information is more likely to be accepted as more time passes since the original incident.

Evaluation of Loftus' research

- Loftus' **studies on leading questions have been accused of being artificial** and too laboratory-based.

- Her first **explanation for the effect of post-event information** was criticised. She claimed that the original memory was replaced by the new, inaccurate memory. More recently, however, Loftus (1991) has agreed with others that **the new, false memory merely obscures the old memory**.

- Her work on leading questions is recognised as important in helping to improve the accuracy of eyewitness testimony.

Fear and anxiety

- Based on his clinical experience, Freud proposed that people forget about some events because they provoke too much anxiety (see page 11). The events, he believed, were so traumatic that they were forced out of consciousness.

- It is obviously unacceptable for researchers to traumatise their participants in order to test the validity of Freud's observations. However, because eyewitnesses who give evidence to the police or the courts are sometimes trying to recall events where they were frightened, researchers have been interested in this area. Loftus (1979) reported the findings of the 'weapon focus' study in which an attempt was made to create an emotionally arousing situation that went some way towards resembling real life.

- A situation was contrived where individual participants, waiting to take part in an experiment, saw a man come out of the laboratory either carrying a pen in greasy hands or carrying a blood-covered paper knife. Later the participants were asked to identify the man from a set of 50 photographs. Only 33% of those in the 'weapon' condition could do so, whereas 49% of those in the 'pen' condition correctly identified the person. Loftus concluded that the anxiety produced by seeing a weapon narrowed what the witness focused on so that they paid less attention to the man's identity.

Evaluation of research on fear and anxiety

- Ethical concerns have been raised by the 'weapon focus' experiment.

- A few other studies have supported Loftus' findings but these studies have exposed participants to only mildly upsetting experiences.

- More recently, Christianson and Hubinette's (1993) research showed that victims of real crimes make more accurate eyewitnesses than bystanders. It appears that people can recall highly stressful events in real life.

Improving eyewitness testimony

The cognitive interview

- Devised by Geiselman et al. (1985), the cognitive interview is a technique used by the police to elicit more accurate information from witnesses. During the interview the witness is encouraged to:
  - **recreate the context** of the original event by imagining the setting (this relates to context-dependent memory)
  - **report every detail** about the incident, no matter how fragmented or apparently irrelevant
  - **recall the event in different orders**, e.g. start part way through and work forwards or back
  - **recall the event from different perspectives** such as imagining what another witness would have seen

- During police interviews with witnesses it is now **standard procedure** to:
  - minimise distractions
  - allow witnesses to proceed at their own pace
  - try to reduce witness anxiety
  - avoid interrupting or leading witnesses

Evaluation of the cognitive interview

- The cognitive interview has been a valuable contribution by cognitive psychologists to enhancing eyewitnesses' recollections and is most effective at improving recall if it is used fairly soon after the event.

- A review of laboratory and field studies (Geiselman and Fisher 1997) found that the cognitive interview produced up to 35% more correct information than the standard interview procedure.

- Other factors improving the accuracy of EWT (Wagstaff 2002):
  - Length of time spent observing event
  - Being close to event observed
  - Good visibility
  - Familiarity of person being observed
  - Novelty or particular relevance of event
  - Short time between witnessing event and recall.

Eyewitness testimony: critical issue

1 What did Bartlett mean when he described memory as reconstructive? (2)

2 Give **two** ways in which schemas can affect memory. (2)

3 Give **one** criticism of schema theory as it has been applied to memory. (1)

4 How did Loftus and Palmer (1974) demonstrate that the wording of a question could affect how fast an eyewitness thought a car was going? (3)

5 When are eyewitnesses unlikely to be misled by leading questions or inaccurate post-event information? (1)

6 Give **two** criticisms of Loftus' research on leading questions. (2)

7 In Loftus' (1979) 'weapon focus' study, what percentage of participants could identify the man who came out of the laboratory carrying either (a) a pen, or (b) a blood-covered paper knife? (2)

8 What explanation did Loftus give for this finding? (1)

9 List **four** factors that are important in improving EWT according to Wagstaff. (2)

10 What are the main cognitive interview techniques used by police to aid accurate recollection of events by witnesses? (4)

Exam tip

When you are asked to 'evaluate', this is not an invitation merely to 'dish the dirt'. Although it is not essential to present both sides of an argument, it is often helpful and positive evaluative points score marks as well as negative evaluations.

The answers are on page 110.

Attachments are special kinds of affectional bonds, where, in addition to desiring closeness, one also feels a sense of comfort and security when with the other person. Kagan et al. (1982) described attachment as 'an intense emotional relationship...enduring over time and in which prolonged separation...is accompanied by stress and sorrow'.

Because the term attachment refers to an internal state it is only by looking at behaviours that we are able to infer its existence. These are called **attachment behaviours** and in young children they include:

- **Seeking proximity** (closeness) to the person to whom one is attached.
- Showing **distress (protest) when separated** from the attachment figure.
- Showing **pleasure when reunited** with the attachment figure.
- Showing a **general orientation towards the person to whom one is attached** (e.g. making eye contact or keeping the person in view).

Parental bonding

- **Attachment is a reciprocal process.** Children become attached to their caregivers (usually parents) and parents become attached to their children. Parents begin to form attachments to their babies (usually called **bonds** in this case) before the babies themselves exhibit attachment behaviours.

- Klaus and Kennell (1976) claimed to have demonstrated in their research that **contact between a mother and her baby during the first few hours after birth** was important if successful bonding was to take place. However, the research was criticised for its methodology. **Subsequent research** has also **failed to support their claims except in the case of mothers who are at above-average risk of failing to bond** (e.g. very young or very poor). In appears that for these mothers there may be some beneficial effects from extended early contact.

- More important for successful bonding by the parent is the development of **synchronised patterns of attachment behaviours** between the child and its parent (Isabella et al. 1989). Schaffer describes these synchronised routines as harmonious interactions in which each person adjusts his/her behaviour in response to the partner's actions. Psychologists have likened these interactions to 'dances' in which partners take turns. As the child and parent become better 'dancers' their relationship becomes more mutually satisfying.

Stages in development of children's attachment

● Schaffer and Emerson (1964) studied 60 infants in Glasgow. They observed them at home and asked mothers to keep records about when their infants showed separation anxiety. They also noted at what ages the infants showed anxiety when approached by an unknown researcher (stranger anxiety). The main findings included:
- Half the children showed their first specific attachment between 6 and 8 months.
- By 18 months only 13% of children were still attached to only one person.
- Attachments were formed to individuals who were responsive and socially interactive with the infant.

● The findings from this longitudinal study led Schaffer and Emerson to propose the following stages in the development of attachment:
- **Pre-attachment** (0–2 months): baby responds socially but indiscriminately towards people.
- **Attachment-in-the-making** (2–7 months): baby can distinguish between familiar and unfamiliar people; shows some preference for familiar people but is comforted by anyone; shows no stranger anxiety.
- **Clear-cut attachment** (7–24 months): baby shows separation protest when attachment figure leaves; shows joy at reunion; fear of strangers peaks between 12–16 months; shows proximity-seeking behaviour (e.g. by crawling to the mother).
- **Multiple attachments** (8 months onwards): after main attachment formed, others follow (e.g. to grandparents).

Evaluation of the stage account

- Subsequent research suggests that infants may be more sociable and more discriminating at an early age than described by Schaffer and Emerson's stages.

- However, there is supporting evidence for the emergence of clear-cut attachment at about 7 months. This coincides and is probably dependent upon the development of object permanence in the infant (knowing that things continue to exist even when they are out of sight). Therefore, when the primary attachment figure leaves, the child is waiting for his/her return and may show separation distress.

- Also at about 7 months babies begin to become mobile (using the attachment figure as a secure base from which to explore). In Uganda, where babies crawl at about 6 months, they also show stranger anxiety at a younger age. Apparently, physical development also plays a part in when clear-cut attachment develops.

- Schaffer and Emerson used observations and mothers' accounts of their babies' behaviour, both methods that are prone to bias. However, the study benefited from being carried out in the children's own homes and avoided the artificiality of a laboratory setting.

Individual differences in children's attachments

The Strange Situation (SS)

- Ainsworth and Bell (1970) studied the quality (security) of children's attachments using a procedure called the Strange Situation (SS). In the SS, observers watch how infants behave during a series of structured episodes that take place in a laboratory setting:
  - Mother brings a child (12–18 months old) into the laboratory, a room where there are attractive toys and comfortable furniture. They look at the toys. A stranger enters the room.
  - Thereafter, a series of episodes occurs in which the child is left alone or left with the stranger. The infant is 'comforted' by the stranger or comforted by its mother if it becomes upset.

- Three types of attachment were identified by Ainsworth and Bell following observations of infants in the SS:
  - **Type A: Avoidant insecure attachment** (15%) – infant is not concerned by mother's absence and avoids contact with her at reunion. Does not prefer mother to the stranger.
  - **Type B: Secure attachment** (70%) – infant explores room when mother is present, is perturbed when she leaves but comforted when she returns. Prefers mother to the stranger.
  - **Type C: Resistant/Ambivalent insecure attachment** (15%) – infant explores very little when mother present and is wary of the stranger; very upset when mother leaves but shows anger when she returns, both seeking and rejecting contact.
  - **Type D: Disorganised insecure attachment** (identified later by Main 1991) – infant appears dazed and confused, showing inconsistent contradictory behaviour.

Explanations for individual differences in attachments

- **Caregiving sensitivity** – warm and consistently loving caregivers are more likely to have securely attached children (Isabella et al. 1989).

- **Child's temperament** – according to Kagan (1982), a child's innate personality may be responsible for the type of attachment it develops. For example, a child who is very easily stressed may develop a resistant insecure attachment.

Evaluation of the SS

- The **reliability** of the SS is high. For example, infants judged in the SS as securely attached were subsequently still found to be securely attached when tested later on in the SS.

- There is also evidence to support the **validity** of the SS (i.e. it measures what it claims to measure). Children identified in the SS as securely attached at 18 months were more popular and showed more initiative and social leadership in later life than insecurely attached infants (Scroufe 1983). This is evidence of **predictive validity**.

- However, some children **responded differently to the SS depending on which parent was present** (Main and Weston 1981). This suggests that the SS measures the quality of the child's **relationship** with its parent rather than a consistent aspect of the child's character.

Cross-cultural variations in attachments

The table summarises the findings from research using the SS in different cultures and shows that a secure attachment is the most common form of attachment in all 8 countries.

Secure and insecure attachments across cultures
(adapted from Van Ijzendoorn and Kroonenberg 1988)

	Percentages to nearest whole number			
	Secure	Avoidant	Resistant	Number of studies
Great Britain	75	22	3	1
West Germany	57	35	8	3
Netherlands	67	26	7	4
Sweden	74	22	4	1
Israel	64	7	29	2
Japan	68	5	27	2
China	50	25	25	1
United States	65	21	14	18

- An Israeli study by Sagi (1990) confirmed Scroufe's findings that securely attached infants develop better social skills later.

- Cross-cultural **differences in child-rearing styles** may explain the differences in types of insecure attachments found. For example, the high levels of distress shown by Japanese infants may not reflect insecure attachment but rather the extreme 'strangeness' of the situation. Therefore, it may be **invalid** to use the SS **measurement** in cultures for which it was not devised (called an imposed etic).

- There are **greater variations** in attachments **within cultures** (e.g. between social classes) than between cultures.

Explanations of attachment

Why do infants become attached? Explanations proposed include learning theory and Bowlby's monotropy theory.

Learning theory

- All behaviours are acquired through conditioning.

- According to classical conditioning principles, food (an unconditioned stimulus) produces pleasure (an unconditioned response). The mother is associated with this pleasure and becomes a conditioned stimulus, which will on its own produce feelings of pleasure. That is, a baby learns to associate its mother with the pleasure it feels when it is fed and consequently seeks to be close to her.

- According to operant conditioning principles, rewarded behaviours are repeated. After feeding, the hunger drive is reduced and this is rewarding. Therefore, when the baby is hungry again it repeats the behaviour (e.g. crying) that leads to drive reduction. Since the mother provides the food to reduce the hunger drive, she becomes a secondary reinforcer (by process of classical conditioning) and the infant strives to stay close to her and thereby becomes attached.

Evaluation of learning theory

- Human infants often become attached to those who do not feed them (Schaffer and Emerson 1964). Earlier, Harlow and Zimmerman's (1959) study of infant monkeys placed with surrogate model mothers found that when the infants were distressed they preferred to cling to a soft model which did not provide food rather than a wire mesh model which did provide food. The supply of food was not enough for attachment to develop.

- The learning theory explanation is highly reductionist, explaining a complex human behaviour in very simple terms.

Bowlby's monotropy theory

Based on his work with children raised in institutions, Bowlby developed his ideas about the importance of attachments if children were to develop normally. He claimed:

- There was a **critical period** (up to age 2.5 years) and if a child did not form a secure attachment during this time it would suffer emotional damage.

- Infants have an innate tendency to form a strong, qualitatively different attachment to **one** individual (monotropy), usually the mother figure.

- This attachment is **adaptive** (increases the infant's chances of survival and reproduction) owing to:
  - **Innate social releasers** (e.g. crying) prompting care-giving from the mother figure.
  - The provision of a **safe base** from which the child can explore.
  - The development of an **internal working model** to act as a template for future relationships (the continuity hypothesis).

Evaluation of Bowlby's theory

- Influential theory with many practical applications for child care.

- Fails to explain why some children cope better than others with unsatisfactory early attachments.

- Evidence that some children can form satisfactory initial attachments after age 2 and a half (see 'Deprivation and privation').

- Does not explain why there is a low correlation between the types of relationships that individual children have (i.e. they tend not to be all the same type, which one would expect if the internal working model was operating as a template for future relationships).

- We cannot know with certainty that the reason why attachment exists is because it is adaptive. This is only an assumption.

Check yourself

Development and variety of attachments

1   Name **two** behaviours that characterise attachment. (2)

2   Name the **four** stages that Schaffer and Emerson identified in the development of children's attachment. (4)

3   What important aspect of cognitive development coincides with the stage when children develop their first specific attachment? (1)

4   Give **one** disadvantage of the method used by Schaffer and Emerson in their Glasgow study of infant attachment. (1)

5   Name the **three** types of attachment identified by Ainsworth and Bell from their studies of infants in the Strange Situation. (3)

6   Give **two** explanations for the individual differences found in the security of children's attachments. (2)

7   Give **one** criticism of the Strange Situation procedure and findings. (1)

8   In which **two** countries did children show the least avoidant insecure attachments? (1)

9   Which **two** processes does learning theory use to explain the development of attachment? (1)

10 Give **one** criticism of the learning theory explanation of attachment development. (1)

11 What did Bowlby mean by a 'critical' period for the development of attachment? (1)

12 What does the term 'monotropy' mean in Bowlby's theory of attachment? (2)

Exam tip

When asked to explain what is meant by two terms (such as 'secure' and 'insecure' attachments for 3+3 marks), it is advisable to explain each term separately and make it clear to the examiner where one explanation ends and the other begins.

The answers are on page 111.

Deprivation

A young child may be separated from one or both caregivers for a variety of reasons, including divorce, death or hospitalisation. When the separation involves the loss of the primary attachment figure and consequent bond disruption, it is called deprivation.

Bowlby's maternal deprivation hypothesis (MDH)

● Bowlby (1953) claimed that the infant and young child, up to the age of 2.5 years, needed to experience a "warm, intimate and continuous relationship with his mother in which both found satisfaction and enjoyment".

● Bowlby's MDH is concerned with the psychological effects of separation. He claimed that if the attachment between infant and mother was broken during the early years (e.g. owing to prolonged separation) and if no substitute mother was available, then the child would be at risk of developing serious emotional and intellectual problems later on.

● Note that not all separations at this time will lead to deprivation. It is only when separation is prolonged or frequent and when no one is available to provide substitute 'mothering' that deprivation occurs and the child is at risk of permanent psychological harm.

Research into the effects of separation

● Robertson and Bowlby (1952) studied the effects on children of brief separation when either their mothers had gone into hospital or when they were hospitalised themselves. They identified three progressive stages that children showed in response to separation:
  ■ Initial protest (lasting several hours or days) – intense period when the child cried a lot and seemed distraught.
  ■ Despair – the child cried less and became apathetic and uninterested in what was happening around it.

- ■ **Detachment** – child was less distressed and appeared to be coping with the separation. However, when the mother reappeared the child showed indifference towards her.

- In one observation study filmed by Robertson and Robertson, a three-year-old boy, John, was separated from his mother for nine days when he attended a residential nursery while she had another baby. For long periods after the separation, John showed hostility towards his mother.

Evaluation of Robertson and Bowlby's early work

- Research showed that even short separations could have long-term detrimental effects upon some children.

- Later research (e.g. Barrett 1997) has shown that the **quality of children's attachments affects their responses to separation**. The less securely attached, the more distressed the child becomes. On the other hand, securely attached children tend to cope quite well with short separations.

- Robertson and Robertson (1971) have also shown that if children are **appropriately prepared** for a short separation they can adjust well. By looking after individual children in their own home when their mothers were going into hospital, the Robertsons demonstrated that bond disruption could be prevented. Preparation for the children included:
  - ■ Visiting the Robertsons' home prior to the separation.
  - ■ Providing a familiar daily routine.
  - ■ Talking to the child about the mother.

It was concluded that in addition to physical care **children who are separated from their mothers also require emotional care**.

- Care of young children in hospitals changed following the findings of Bowlby and the Robertsons. Parents are now encouraged to stay in hospital with their young children.

Research into the effects of deprivation

- Bowlby's 'study of 44 thieves' provided the kind of evidence that led him to formulate his maternal deprivation hypothesis.
  - He compared 44 child thieves with 44 other maladjusted children (who had committed no crimes).
  - He labelled 32% of the thieves 'affectionless psychopaths' because they lacked any sense of guilt or remorse.
  - None of the non-thieves was classed as affectionless psychopaths. 86% of the affectionless psychopaths had experienced 'early and prolonged separation from their mothers' compared with very few of the other children he studied.

- Evaluation of Bowlby's '44 thieves study':
  - Data about separations may not have been reliable because it was collected retrospectively (after the event).
  - Children who experienced separations probably suffered multiple deprivations, not just the loss of the attachment figure.
  - The diagnosis of affectionless psychopathy was made by Bowlby himself and so may have been influenced by his own expectations.
  - Relationship between psychopathy and separation is correlational. One cannot claim that separation caused the children to steal.
  - Rutter et al. (1976) studied young boys on the Isle of Wight and found that family discord, rather than separation, was related to behavioural problems and emotional maladjustment.
  - It is not clear which children experienced deprivation through separation and which experienced privation (the lack of an opportunity to form any attachment).

- Bowlby et al. (1956) looked at the effects of separation on children who had been sent away from home to be treated for tuberculosis when they were under 4 years old. Visited weekly by their parents, they showed no more problems later in childhood than a control (comparison) group of children who had not been sent away.

- Evidence from a longitudinal study of 5000 children revealed that children who have been hospitalised under the age of 4 years for extended periods are more likely to have behavioural problems and reading difficulties in adolescence (Douglas 1975). However, Clarke and Clarke (1976) have pointed out that it is poorer children who tend to spend more time in hospital. Their home environments, therefore, might explain their later problems rather than the separations they experienced during their hospital stays.

Privation

Privation refers to the lack (rather than the loss) of an attachment. The effects of privation, according to Rutter (1981), are more long-lasting and severe than the effects of deprivation or mere separation.

Effects of privation: evidence from case studies

- Genie (Curtiss 1989) was the victim of severe neglect and abuse. When she was discovered at age 13 and a half years, she had no language and could hardly walk. After nurturing and educational help, Genie made progress but has never achieved normal language or social skills. This might have been caused by her isolation, by poor-quality after-care or by some personal characteristic of Genie.

- Freud and Dann (1951), however, reported more encouraging outcomes from their study of six war orphans. While the children were still infants, their parents had died in a concentration camp. They received little adult care but they grew very attached to each other during the time they spent together until they were taken to England at the end of the Second World War. Eventually, the children did form attachments to adults and their social and language development was rapid.

- Koluchova (1976) reported the case of Czech twin boys who were neglected and abused by their father and stepmother. They were discovered at age 7 when they could hardly walk, had very poor speech and were easily frightened. After good-quality hospital and foster care they made excellent cognitive and social progress.

Evaluation of case study evidence

● Case studies provide insights into exceptional cases that could not be studied in any other way. However, evidence is often gathered from unstructured interviews, is retrospective and therefore prone to distortions in memory. The contents of case reports are inevitably selective and one cannot make generalisations from a single case study.

Effects of privation: evidence from studies of institutionalisation

● Hodges and Tizard (1989) carried out a longitudinal investigation of 65 children placed in institutional care before the age of 4 months. The children suffered privation. By the age of 4 years, 24 children had been adopted, 15 had been restored to their original families and 26 stayed in the institution. (Therefore, this study took the form of a natural experiment.) The children were assessed at 4, 8 and 16 years of age.
   ■ Adopted children formed the closest attachments (to their adoptive parents) and 'restored' children had less good relationships with their natural parents.
   ■ Compared with a control group, both the adopted and restored children tended to crave adult attention and approval and were less socially successful.

● Hodges and Tizard concluded that children adopted into loving homes partially overcame the detrimental effects of privation, e.g. in their relationships with those who were willing to make special efforts. However, in situations such as school, problems emerged.

Evaluation of evidence from studies of institutionalisation

   ■ Some children dropped out of the study before the end. Therefore, the final sample of 42, from whose behaviour conclusions were drawn, might have been biased.
   ■ Within both the adopted and the 'restored' groups of children there were individual differences. For example, some adoptive families were not particularly good and some 'restored' families were better than others.

Check yourself

Deprivation and privation

1 Define deprivation. (1)
2 Define privation. (1)
3 Name and describe the **three** stages that children show in response to separation (according to Bowlby and Robertson). (6)
4 According to Bowlby and Robertson, what should parents and hospitals strive to prevent if young children have to be separated from their parents? (1)
5 Explain Bowlby's maternal deprivation hypothesis. (1)
6 In Bowlby's study of '44 thieves', what percentage were classified as 'affectionless psychopaths'? (1)
7 What percentage of those classified as 'affectionless psychopaths' had experienced early, prolonged separation? (1)
8 Why do you think that the children sent away from home before the age of 4 because they had tuberculosis experienced no long-term detrimental social or emotional effects? (2)
9 Bowlby's maternal deprivation hypothesis offers one explanation for the later problems faced by children who have had many or prolonged stays in hospital during early childhood. What other explanation do Clarke and Clarke offer? (1)
10 Name (cite) **one** case study of a child/children who suffered severe privation. (1)
11 In the longitudinal study by Hodges and Tizard, how many children were in the sample (a) at the start, and (b) at the end of the study? (2)
12 Summarise the **two** main conclusions drawn from Hodges and Tizard's study. (2)

Exam tip

If you are asked to describe aspects of **one** study (e.g. findings and conclusions), make sure you stick to **one** study. If, for example, you give findings from more than one study you will waste time and be credited for only one study's findings anyway.

The answers are on pages 111–12.

'Day care' refers to the care of children by people other than the children's parents. The care is usually (though not always) provided outside the child's own home and includes nursery schools, day nurseries and childminding. Psychologists are interested in:
- The **cognitive and social effects** of day care.
- Ways of **improving** day-care provision.

Research into the cognitive effects of day care

Cognitive development is the development of thinking (e.g. the ability to reason, use language and solve problems).

Nursery schools and day nurseries

- Kagan et al. (1980) compared 33 children who were full-time attenders at a well-run **nursery school** with a comparison group of children who were **cared for at home** by their mothers.
  - No consistent differences were found between the two groups.
  - Kagan et al. concluded that this form of **day care had no detrimental effects on the children's cognitive development**.

- Andersson (1992) conducted a longitudinal study of over 100 Swedish children from a variety of home backgrounds. Some attended **day nurseries** and some were cared for at home. At ages 8 and 13 years, the children were assessed by their teachers and by IQ tests.
  - Academic (cognitive) **performance was best in the children who had entered day care before age 1**. Boys especially benefited.
  - Cognitive achievement was poorest among the children who received no day care.
  - However, the children who experienced day care tended also to come from more affluent homes and their **privileged backgrounds might explain their better school performances**. Nevertheless, day care had no detrimental effects on these children.

- Another study reported by Andersson, but carried out in Texas, USA, found that **day care was linked with negative effects on later school performance**. Two possible explanations are:

- The **better quality** of day care provided in Sweden compared with that on offer in Texas.
- The **difference in parental leave systems** between Sweden and Texas. Before returning to work, Swedish parents have more time than Texan parents to form strong, secure attachments with their children before they are placed in day care.

● The National Institute of Child Health and Human Development (NICHD) Study of Early Child Care (1997) is a large-scale study of over 1300 infants and their families in the USA. The families are drawn from a wide variety of backgrounds. The study found small but significant **positive effects of good-quality day care on children's cognitive skills**, including their language. The effect was most positive for children from poor backgrounds.

Childminding

● Bryant et al. (1980) and Mayall and Petrie (1983) found that the **quality of care offered by childminders varied considerably**. While some provided good-quality care others failed to stimulate the children and were more concerned with keeping the children quiet than with enhancing their development.

● Broberg et al. (1997) compared the cognitive development of 8-year-old children who had experienced nursery care, or childminding, or staying at home. **Those who had been in nursery care developed the best verbal and mathematical abilities. Those who had been cared for by childminders fared worst.**

Operation Head Start

● Operation Head Start (HS) was designed in the 1960s as a preschool enrichment programme to help disadvantaged American children from impoverished backgrounds. Initial results from when the children entered school were promising, but the benefits shown at first by the HS children, compared with comparable children who had not been on a preschool enrichment programme, soon disappeared.

- Later follow-up research (e.g. by Lazar and Darlington 1982), however, has shown that the HS children were eventually more likely to attend college and less likely to experience social problems than children from comparable backgrounds who had not received preschool educational day care.

Research into social effects of day care

Effects on attachments

According to Bowlby's line of argument, separating young children from their parents by placing children in day care might have detrimental effects on their later emotional and social development. This will occur if the separation interferes with forming or maintaining initial attachments.

- Belsky and Rovine (1988) tested babies using the strange situation and found that day care had detrimental effects on attachments. Most research, however, has revealed no weakening of attachments in children who were separated from their mothers when attending day care.

- Clarke-Stewart et al. (1994) studied 500 children. They found no difference in attachment between the children who had experienced 30 hours of day care per week from 3 months old and the children who had experienced only 10 hours per week.

- The NICHD Study of Early Child Care (1997) reported that child care per se was unrelated to the security of a child's attachment. However, where children were exposed to both insensitive mothers and poor-quality day care they were at greater risk of developing insecure attachment.

Other social effects

- In Andersson's (1992) Swedish study, children who experienced day care showed greater socio-emotional competence than those who had stayed at home.

- Shea (1981) videotaped 3- and 4-year-olds in a nursery playground. The children's sociability increased over the first 10 weeks they spent at the nursery, especially among the children who attended 5 days per week.

- Clarke-Stewart et al. (1994) found in their study of Chicago children that those who attended day nurseries were more **socially advanced in dealing with their peers** than those who stayed at home.

- Bates et al. (1994), however, found most **aggressive behaviour** among school children who had spent most time in day care. The reason for this apparently conflicting finding may lie in the quality of day care experienced. Research shows that **children's aggression levels are lower if they spend their time in well-structured, stimulating environments whether these are in or out of the child's own home.**

Summing up the evidence

- Most evidence to date suggests that **children in day care are not disadvantaged in their cognitive or social development.**

- **Children from poor backgrounds benefit most**, both cognitively and socially, from good-quality day care (Scarr 1998). Stimulating day care appears to compensate for what is missing in impoverished homes.

- Poor-quality day care, however, **aggravates problems with attachment** for children who also have insensitive mothers.

What comprises good-quality day care?

- **Stability and consistency:** Low staff turnover and low staff–child ratios help produce consistency of care to enable children to form attachments to their carers.

- **Well-trained staff:** Howes et al. (1998) reported the beneficial effects of providing in-service training to improve the sensitivity of caregivers.

- **Warm and responsive interactions** between the staff and the children.

- **Limited group size** to allow lots of verbal interaction between the caregivers and the children.

- **Sufficient resources** (toys, book etc.) and space to provide a stimulating environment.

Day care: critical issue

1 Define day care. (1)

2 Give **three** examples of types of day care found in the UK. (3)

3 What conclusion did Kagan et al. draw from their 1980 study of children in full-time nursery school? (1)

4 Give **two** findings from Andersson's Swedish study. (2)

5 What factor, other than day care, might explain the findings from Andersson's study? (1)

6 Which type of day care has been shown to be least helpful in stimulating children's cognitive abilities? (1)

7 What is Operation Head Start? (1)

8 Why might Bowlby have been cautious about young children receiving day care? (2)

9 In a sentence, sum up the main conclusion from research on the effect of day care on attachment development. (1)

10 Name (cite) **one** study that has demonstrated positive social effects of day care. (1)

11 For which group of children does poor-quality day care seem to have particularly detrimental effects on their attachments? (1)

12 Give **five** features of good-quality day care. (5)

Exam tip

Remember, if a question asks you to describe research findings in a particular area, you need to describe **more than one finding**, although the findings can be from one piece of research. Don't waste time on giving details of procedures. These will earn no marks.

The answers are on pages 112–13.

We experience **stress** when we are in situations where the demands made on us seem greater than our ability to cope. A common definition of stress is **'a state of psychological tension and physiological arousal caused by something (a stressor) in the environment'**. This definition focuses on the **response** or **reaction** of the person.

The body's response to stressors

When your brain detects a stressor it triggers an **alarm reaction**, which prepares the body for action (sometimes called the 'fight or flight response'). Two systems are involved in this reaction.

- The **autonomic nervous system.**
- The **endocrine system.**

The autonomic nervous system (ANS)

The ANS is part of the body's nervous system. The nervous system is divided into two main parts:

- **The central nervous system (CNS)** – the brain and the spinal cord. The **hypothalamus**, part of the CNS and situated deep within the brain, is important in relation to stress because it **controls the pituitary gland** that is situated just below it.

- **The peripheral nervous system (PNS)** – all the other nerve cells in the body. The PNS divides into two parts. The **somatic nervous system** – concerned with voluntary movements. The **autonomic nervous system (ANS)** – concerned with the **control of involuntary functions** of the body (those functions that work without you having to think about them). This part of the nervous system is **particularly important in how we respond to stressors**.

The **ANS** maintains the functioning of such systems as digestion, heart rate and blood flow. It has two subdivisions:

- **The sympathetic branch** – activates the body to cope with emergencies (e.g. increases heart rate and respiration).
- **The parasympathetic branch** – calms the body and conserves energy (e.g. decreases heart rate and respiration).

The ANS arouses or quietens bodily systems via the hormones released by the endocrine system.

The endocrine system

The endocrine system consists of glands that secrete hormones that are carried by the bloodstream to other body organs.

● The **hypothalamus plays a central role** in controlling the endocrine system. When a stressor is perceived, the hypothalamus **stimulates the anterior pituitary gland** to produce the hormone ACTH, which in turn stimulates the adrenal cortex (the outer layer of the adrenal glands, situated just above the kidneys) to produce corticosteroids such as glucocorticoids. This system is called the **hypothalamic-pituitary-adrenal axis**.

● The **hypothalamus** also activates the sympathetic branch of the ANS by **stimulating the adrenal medulla** (the inner core of the adrenal glands) to produce adrenaline and noradrenaline in times of stress. This system is called the **sympatho-adrenomedullary axis**.

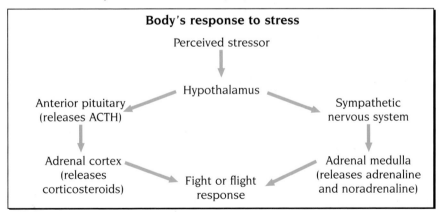

Body's response to stress

Perceived stressor

Hypothalamus

Anterior pituitary
(releases ACTH)

Sympathetic
nervous system

Adrenal cortex
(releases
corticosteroids)

Fight or flight
response

Adrenal medulla
(releases adrenaline
and noradrenaline)

The General Adaptation Syndrome (GAS)

It is normal to experience stress. Sometimes people even go out of their way to experience it (e.g. taking part in dangerous sports). A degree of stress is good for us. It keeps us alert and motivates us to act (e.g. to revise for examinations). However, prolonged and unwanted stress may cause physical and psychological harm. Selye (1956) proposed the GAS to explain both the **short-term bodily effects** of exposure to stressors and also **how prolonged stress reactions could lead to physical illness.**

The three stages of Selye's GAS

1   **Alarm reaction stage** – stress-response systems activated, e.g. pituitary secretes ACTH and the adrenal medulla secretes adrenaline.

2   **Resistance stage** – the body is adapting to cope with the stressor but the organism is increasingly susceptible to disease or injury.

3   **Exhaustion stage** – if the stressor continues then ultimately the body's ability to cope with it and other stressors starts to fail and exhaustion sets in. This may result in damage to the body's immune system, the development of stress-related diseases or, in extreme situations, death.

Evaluation of Selye's GAS

● The GAS is based on Seyle's animal work carried out in the 1930s. He subjected rats to a range of physical stressors and noted their reactions. By today's standards his work seems cruel and **unethical.** However, it did lead to the **recognition that there was a relationship between stress and physical illness.**

● Probably because his **early work was based on non-human animals** Selye focused on physiological factors. However, his later work acknowledged **the importance of cognitive and emotional factors.**

● The 'general' element of the GAS has been challenged. Some physiologists claim there may be different physiological responses to different stressors and therefore charge the theory with **oversimplifying** the processes involved.

Stress and physical illness

There is considerable evidence to link stress with illness. Stress can adversely affect the body **directly or indirectly.**

Some direct effects

● If the energy mobilised as part of the stress response is not burnt up, then dangerously high levels of glucose and fatty acids remain in the bloodstream and increase the risk of cardiovascular disease.

● During the body's stress response, blood pressure increases, resulting in the lining of **blood vessels being damaged**. Where scarring occurs there is an increased risk of plaques (fatty deposits) developing and blocking the blood vessel. If these plaques rupture they may block the blood supply to the heart and cause the death of some tissue.

● Elevated levels of corticosteroids increase risks of arthritis.

● The corticosteroids released during the stress response can **damage the immune system**, e.g. by preventing the growth of T cells. The endorphins (body's natural pain killers), released at times of stress, may protect us from pain but they also suppress immune functioning.

The immune system

The immune system protects the body from infection by recognising and destroying foreign substances (antigens) such as bacteria and cancer cells. Among the cells in the immune system are:
● **T cells** – work to destroy antigens in cells of the body.
● **B cells** – produce antibodies that bind to antigens and kill them while they are still in the bloodstream.
● **Natural killer (NK) cells** – fight against tumours.

Some indirect effects

● Stress may lead people to **behave in ways that increase their chances of becoming ill**, e.g. they may increase their consumption of alcohol and reduce the amount of exercise they take.

● Johnson (1986) reported that stress results in **increased numbers of accidents** at home, at work and in the car.

Research into the relationship between stress and physical illness

Stress and cardiovascular disorders

- Cobb and Rose (1973) found a **significant relationship** between hypertension (consistently high blood pressure) and the degree of stress experienced by air traffic controllers. Hypertension is a risk factor for coronary heart disease (CHD).

- Rahe et al. (1974) investigated the link between CHD and stress in 400 Finnish CHD patients. Some had survived and some had died. Life-change data collected from the patients or their relatives showed that prior to the patients' illness, they had experienced an increase in stressful life events. However, this was a **retrospective study** and people's memories for events might not be reliable.

- A **prospective study** (Byrne et al. 1981) interviewed 120 men and women who had survived heart attacks about their worries. Eight months later the survivors were located. Patients who had died or suffered a recurrence of their illness had reported more worries at the first interview than those who remained well. However, the study **does not provide a causal link** between CHD and stress as other factors (e.g. relating to personality) might explain both the recurrences of the disease and the reported worries.

- Friedman and Rosenmann (1974) found that people who were **time-pressured, highly competitive and prone to anger and hostility were more at risk of CHD than those who were more relaxed**. They called this high-risk way of behaving **Type A behaviour**. They found that 70% of those with CHD were classified as Type A. Later studies have found moderate correlations between Type A behaviour and CHD. Reanalysis of Friedman and Rosenmann's findings has revealed that it is the **hostility** component of Type A behaviour that is associated with CHD. High levels of hostility lead to increased activity in the sympathetic nervous system. Behaviour modification programmes to change Type A behaviours have been successful in preventing recurrence of CHD (Friedman et al. 1986).

Stress and the immune system

Some research claims to have demonstrated that stress **directly affects immune functioning**:

- Kiecolt-Glaser et al. (1984) studied medical students before and during their exams. Using blood samples, they found that the students' immune systems were suppressed (reduced) once the exam period began. The use of a **real-life**, long-lasting stressor (exams) is a strength in this study.

- Immunosuppression has also been found among unhappily married women, recently bereaved spouses and those who have cared long term for Alzheimer patients. These are **correlational findings**, however, and so one cannot assume that the stressful circumstances caused the lowered immune functioning.

- Cohen et al. (1993) asked volunteers to answer questions so that their psychological stress index could be calculated. Volunteers were then exposed to a cold virus. Those with high stress scores developed more colds than did those with low stress scores. The use of **direct measures** helped to establish cause and effect relationships between stress and increased vulnerability to disease.

Stress is associated with risky behaviours and so may suppress immune systems **indirectly**:

- Opiates depress the immune system. Therefore those who resort to opiate abuse as a means of escaping stressful situations are prone to develop infections (Sheridan 1992).

- Adolescents are more likely to start smoking if they are experiencing high levels of stress (Wells 1985).

- People who have given up smoking but who subsequently suffer high levels of stress are more likely to resume smoking than those who experience less stress (Carey et al. 1993).

Check yourself

Stress as a bodily response

1 What is the fight or flight response? (3)

2 Give the names and functions of the **two** subdivisions of the autonomic nervous system (ANS). (4)

3 What is the role of the hypothalamus in the body's stress response? (4)

4 Name the **three** stages of Selye's General Adaptation Syndrome (GAS). (3)

5 Give **one** criticism of the theory of the GAS. (1)

6 Give **one** way in which stress might directly damage the immune system. (1)

7 In Friedman and Rosenmann's study of CHD patients, what percentage was classified as displaying Type A behaviour? (1)

8 Which aspect of Type A behaviour is most strongly associated with coronary heart disease (CHD)? (1)

9 Which stressor did Kiecolt-Glaser use when she looked at the relationship between stress and immune functioning in medical students? (1)

10 In what way might stress indirectly cause illness? (1)

Exam tip

In the exam it is important to **use your time effectively**. You are required to answer two questions in one hour, i.e. 30 minutes per question. Allow a couple of minutes to read all questions carefully and decide which ones you are going to answer. Spend no more than 5 minutes on each of parts (a) and (b). Part (c) is worth 18 marks and is the trickiest part to answer. You will need 18–20 minutes to answer it well.

The answers are on page 113.

There are many perceived sources of stress that have been researched in a number of different ways. For example, life events, everyday hassles, aspects of the workplace and individual differences have been investigated.

Life events and stress

● Two doctors, Holmes and Rahe (1967), noticed that their patients often seemed to have experienced several life events prior to the onset of illness. This led them to suggest that life events, such as divorce or bereavement, forced people to change, causing them stress and making them more susceptible to illness.

● To test this hypothesis, they developed the Social Readjustment Rating Scale (SRRS), which consists of 43 life events. Each event was rated by hundreds of participants as to the amount of adjustment it required. Ratings were averaged and each event was scored (given a stress value) in life change units (LCUs).

● Death of a spouse was assigned the highest value of 100 LCUs, marriage 53 LCUs and Christmas 12 LCUs. As you see, even positive events involve adjustment and so can cause stress.

● To administer the SRRS, individuals simply tick the events that have affected them over the last year or two and total the LCUs for the items ticked.

● Holmes and Rahe found positive correlations between high SRRS scores and risk of physical or mental illness. Other researchers have also found modest but significant associations.

Evaluation of research using the SRRS

● Research is correlational and so we cannot assume that stress (caused by life events) really causes illness. In some cases the illness may have preceded and even caused the life event.

● Scale values are arbitrary and likely to differ from person to person (e.g. some people find Christmas more stressful than others).

- The SRRS has been criticised for **not distinguishing between positive and negative life events**.

- Scores depend on **self-reports** and these are notoriously unreliable.

- However, the SRRS has been widely used and was **an important step in attempting to quantify levels of stress**.

- Not only major life events cause stress. Everyday events can also be stressful. These are called daily hassles.

Hassles and uplifts

- **Hassles** are **defined** as 'irritating, frustrating, distressing demands that to some degree characterise everyday transactions with the environment'.

- Kanner et al. (1981) devised the **Hassles Scale**, originally a list of 117 items, to measure people's experience of day-to-day stressful events (e.g. rising prices, having too much to do). Participants indicate which hassles have been experienced in the past month and rate their severity.

- Because hassles often seem to be more tolerable if good things are happening at the same time, an **Uplifts Scale** was devised. It consisted of 135 items that bring feelings of satisfaction and joy and was administered in the same way as the Hassles Scale.

- Frequently occurring uplifts include relating well to a spouse or partner, completing a task, getting enough sleep and feeling healthy.

- De Longis et al. (1982) found stronger **correlations between scores on the Hassles Scale and health status** than between SRRS scores and health. Uplifts scores did not correlate with health status.

Workplace stressors

Most people experience work-related stress at some time. Stressors inherent in the job (e.g. having responsibility for other people's lives) might cause this. So also might the environment where one works (e.g. noisy or crowded).

Lack of control

When people have little control over the pace or procedures in their jobs (e.g. assembly-line workers) **they experience stress.**

- Langer and Rodin (1976) reported that residents living in a home for the elderly were happier, more active and lived longer if they were given control over some aspects of their lives (e.g. whether or not to have visitors, looking after a plant if they wished). Some judgements by staff about the residents' states of well-being have been criticised as subjective. Nevertheless, the study supports the claim that **personal control can reduce stress and improve health**.

- Johansson et al. (1978) found that Swedish sawmill workers whose job was machine-paced (they had no control), monotonous and isolating had high levels of stress-related health problems.

- Marmot et al.'s (1997) longitudinal study of civil servants showed that those on low grades (with little control) were more likely to have heart attacks than were those on higher grades.

- However, Brady's (1958) 'executive' monkey experiment demonstrated that monkeys who could avoid receiving shocks by pressing a lever were more likely to develop gastric ulcers than those who had no control over the shocks being given. It seems, therefore, that if **responsibilities** (to control situations) **are too onerous and long-lasting they may lead to adverse effects**. However, we need to be cautious when generalising from studies using non-human animals.

The physical environment

- **Noisy or crowded conditions**, for example, are associated with stress.

- Glass et al. (1969) found that **random noise was more stressful than predictable noise** and led to worse performance on cognitive tasks. The best performance, however, occurred in quiet conditions.

- Cohen et al. (1981) compared children attending noisy schools with those attending quiet schools. The children at the noisy schools had higher blood pressure and more problems with concentration.

- Studies have shown that **crowding becomes stressful when it reduces people's feelings of control** and eventually impairs their ability to cope.

Other factors related to stress in the workplace

- **Demands of the task:** excessive workloads are associated with increased rates of ill health and accidents; boring jobs that fail to use a worker's abilities also produce stress (Quick and Quick 1984).

- **Responsibility for people's lives:** health professionals and those who work in the emergency services report feelings of **burnout**, i.e. exhaustion, loss of identity and feelings of inadequacy.

- **Role ambiguity:** when there are insufficient guidelines about what one should be doing or aiming for in one's job uncertainty and stress result.

- **Poor interpersonal relationships:** social support from fellow workers is an important ingredient for job satisfaction and so it is not surprising that poor relationships contribute to job stress.

- **Perceived inadequate recognition or advancement:** workers experience stress if they feel passed over for promotion.

- **Job insecurity:** the threat of unemployment is stressful particularly if there is little chance of finding other work.

- **Shift work:** disruption caused to sleeping patterns can be stressful and contribute to workplace accidents.

Individual differences

Personality

- As already discussed, individuals with **Type A** behaviour are more stressed than those who are more relaxed (see p.42 for more detail).

- The term '**Type C personality**' (proposed by Temshok 1987) describes those who have difficulty in expressing emotion. These characteristics have been linked with **cancer progression** (but not with its cause).

- **Hardiness**: Kobasa coined the term 'hardiness' to describe the attributes possessed by people who cope well with stressful situations. The three characteristics of hardiness are:
  - **Control** – belief in one's ability to control one's life.
  - **Commitment** – sense of involvement in life's activities.
  - **Challenge** – seeing changes as opportunities rather than as threat.

Kobasa's own research findings support the link between hardiness and better health. However, there are **problems in assessing hardiness** and there is **little research on how people become hardy**.

Gender

- During stressful situations, **men show greater increases in blood pressure and stress hormones** than women do. This might be caused by physiological differences or it might reflect the different ways that men and women appraise (judge) stressful situations.

- It has been suggested that if men are physiologically more reactive to stress than women this might explain why men are more susceptible to CHD. However, other factors may also be important. Women lead healthier lives, take fewer risks and make more use of social support networks at times of stress than men do. Women also display less Type A behaviour.

Culture

- Stress is experienced in all cultures but some cultures place a greater emphasis on competitiveness, working hard and being successful. Margolis et al. (1995) found that Type A behaviour was more common in such cultures.

- Triandis (1995) suggests that those who live in more **collectivist cultures support each other more** and so cope better with stressful situations. Research in the US has found that Asian- and African-Americans use social support networks of family and friends more than white Americans for coping with stress.

Check yourself

Sources of stress

1 What did Holmes and Rahe mean by 'life events'? (2)

2 What is the SRRS? (2)

3 Which life event was given the highest stress value and what value was assigned to it? (2)

4 Give **two** criticisms of the research using the SRRS Scale. (2)

5 Which scale was devised alongside the Hassles Scale as a way of measuring positive, cheerful events? (1)

6 How is the Hassles Scale administered? (2)

7 Give the **two** main findings of DeLongis et al.'s study into the relationship between hassles and health. (2)

8 What conclusion was drawn from Langer and Rodin's study of elderly people living in a residential home? (1)

9 How did the findings of Brady's 'executive' monkey experiment differ from those of other studies that have investigated effects of control on the experience of stress? (2)

10 When does crowding become stressful? (1)

11 What characterises 'burnout'? (3)

Exam tip

When you are asked to outline or describe something for 3 marks (e.g. 'Describe one physiological approach to stress management'), try to: **I**dentify what you are describing; **E**xplain what it is/means; provide an **E**xample. This **IEE** approach should help you gain the 3 marks.

The answers are on pages 113–14.

To manage stress we need to:
- Adopt a lifestyle that **reduces the potential for stress** (e.g. learn how to relax, develop good social support networks).
- Find ways of **reducing the strain caused by the stressors we encounter** (e.g. use anti-anxiety drugs, biofeedback or training programmes to overcome specific stressors).

Physical methods of managing negative effects of stress

Drugs

During times of stress the body produces hormones that create anxiety. Drugs have been developed to counteract this anxiety. They include:

- **Barbiturates:** barbiturates depress central nervous system activity, but they produce serious side effects, including addiction.

- **Benzodiazepines (BZs):** widely used and highly effective at reducing anxiety, BZs (e.g. Valium) reduce the activity of serotonin, one of the brain's neurotransmitters. Side effects include drowsiness, impaired memory and dependency.

- **Beta-blockers:** reduce activity in the sympathetic nervous system, lowering heart rate and blood pressure. Like all drugs, beta-blockers only treat the symptoms (not the cause) of stress.

Biofeedback

- **Biofeedback** involves recording physiological activity, such as heart rate or muscle tension, usually by placing electrodes on the body. The information is fed back to the individual via a monitor. Using learned relaxation techniques, the individual tries, for example, to reduce muscle tension in the neck and receives feedback from the recordings as to whether or not this has been achieved.

- **Biofeedback is based on the principles of operant conditioning.** Behaviour (in this case, relaxing) that is rewarded (i.e. seen on the monitor to reduce muscle tension) will be repeated.

- Biofeedback has been used to help people suffering from chronic tension headaches and Reynaud's disease where restricted blood flow to the fingers and toes causes extreme pain.

- Biofeedback seems to be more successful with children than with adults, probably because children are more enthusiastic and approach it as a game (Attanasio et al. 1985).

- Hatch et al. (1982) think that claims for biofeedback are exaggerated and that relaxation procedures without biofeedback are just as successful at reducing stress. Furthermore, the technique is expensive and time-consuming.

Psychological approaches

Progressive muscle relaxation

- This is an active way of reducing bodily arousal. The individual focuses on specific muscle groups (starting, e.g., with those in the feet and working up through the body), alternately tightening and relaxing them until the sensations of tension and relaxation are understood. A quick version of the procedure can then be used in real-life stressful situations.

- Relaxation techniques can be beneficial in some situations but where stressors are long-lasting and severe, a more focused approach that addresses the source of stress is needed.

Cognitive-behavioural therapies

The **transactional model** of stress defines it as **'a lack of fit between the perceived demands of the environment and the perceived ability to cope with those demands'**. That is, the way we **appraise** (judge) situations plays an important role in whether or not we experience the psychological state of 'being stressed'. Cognitive-behavioural therapies address both aspects of the transactional definition. They aim to **modify the perceived demands** of potentially stressful situations by a process of cognitive restructuring, and **improve the coping skills** of individuals when they are faced with stressors.

● **Rational emotive therapy (RET)** (Ellis 1962) is based on the view that stress is often caused by **irrational thinking** that leads one to appraise situations as threatening and therefore stressful. RET aims to challenge and change irrational thoughts. According to Ellis' **ABC model**, irrational self-defeating thoughts lead to anxiety and poor functioning:
  ■ A – **Activating** event (e.g. failed an exam).
  ■ B – **Beliefs** (about why one failed, e.g. 'because I'm stupid').
  ■ C – **Consequences** flowing from B (e.g. leaving college).

RET involves adding steps D and E
  ■ D – therapist **disputes** (challenges) the irrational beliefs.
  ■ E – the **effect** of D is to restructure the person's beliefs about him/herself.

Evaluation: RET has been fairly effective in treating anger and anxiety, but there are difficulties in measuring 'irrational beliefs' and doubts about whether improvements are lasting.

● **Stress inoculation training (SIT)** (Meichenbaum 1977) teaches people skills to cope with stress and to achieve personal goals. There are **three** phases to the training:
  ■ **Conceptualisation** (cognitive element) – assess the nature of the problem and how it might be remedied.
  ■ **Skills training practice** (behavioural element) – stress-reduction techniques (e.g. relaxation); behavioural skills (e.g. of communication); cognitive techniques (e.g. positive self-talk).
  ■ **Real-life applications** – use learned skills in role-play then in the real world; attend follow-up sessions.

Evaluation:
  ■ SIT deals with both the sources of stress and how to deal with it.
  ■ SIT training can be generalised from one situation to help with other potentially stressful situations.

- Some people find it difficult to use positive self-talk (e.g. 'just keep calm, you can do it').
- SIT is time-consuming and expensive.

● **Hardiness training:** Kobasa has shown that 'hardiness' is associated with health (see page 49). Kobasa's (1986) programme of training involves **three** techniques to enhance hardiness:
  - **Focusing:** become aware of physical signs of stress (e.g. muscle tension in the neck) and identify the cause.
  - **Reconstructing stress situations:** think about a recent stressful situation and make two lists: how it could have worked out better and how it could have worked out worse. Aims to encourage a more positive attitude by showing that things could have been worse.
  - **Compensating through self-improvement:** undertake challenges where one can succeed in order to build up confidence.

Evaluation:
  - Lengthy training that requires commitment.
  - Limited evidence of success but some reports (e.g. Sarafino 1990) that training leads to improved hardiness scores, feeling less stressed and reduced blood pressure.

● **Use of social support:** social support refers to the **perceived comfort, caring, esteem or help a person receives from other people or groups** (Wallston et al. 1983). Research findings suggest that social support reduces the stress that people experience and benefits health (e.g. LaRocco et al. 1980).There are **two** explanations offered for how social support influences health and well-being:
  - **The buffering hypothesis:** social support protects the person against negative effects of stress, e.g. by helping them appraise stressful situations more optimistically because they can expect help.
  - **The direct effects hypothesis:** social support benefits health and well-being regardless of the amount of stress people are facing, e.g. by enhancing their self-esteem.

Evaluation: social support usually reduces stress and benefits health. There are times, however, when this is not the case, e.g., if one's social support network sets a bad example by engaging in unhealthy behaviours such as smoking and excessive drinking.

Role of control in relation to stress

As discussed on page 47, people may experience stress when they lack a sense of control. Indeed, personal control is an important part of hardiness. When Langer and Rodin gave small increases in personal control to elderly people in a residential home, their health and life expectancy improved.

Locus of control

● People with a strong **external locus of control** feel that 'things happen to them' and that life is largely uncontrollable (Rotter 1966). They tend to suffer more stress-related illnesses and are poorer at coping than people who have an **internal locus of control** (believe that what happens to them is largely under their own control).

● An external locus of control, however, is **difficult to change**.

● Nevertheless, **giving people an illusion of control can sometimes reduce stress**. Glass and Singer (1972), for example, found that people exposed to uncontrollable noise but given the illusion of control by having a button to press (which had no effect on the noise) showed less measurable stress response than those exposed to the noise but given no button to press.

Self-efficacy

● Another aspect of personal control is one's sense of self-efficacy – a **belief that one can succeed** at something (Bandura 1977).

● Those with a strong sense of self-efficacy manage stress better than those with a weak sense of self-efficacy.

● If cognitive-behavioural programmes, such as SIT, are successful they should enhance a person's sense of self-efficacy.

Check yourself

Stress management: critical issue

1 Name **one** type of anti-anxiety drug used to manage stress. (1)

2 Give **one** criticism made of drug treatments for coping with stress. (1)

3 Give **one** criticism of biofeedback as a means of managing stress. (1)

4 What are the **two** general aims of cognitive-behavioural treatments for stress? (2)

5 What view did Ellis hold about the cause of stress that underlies his Rational Emotive Therapy (RET)? (1)

6 In RET what do the initials ABC stand for? (3)

7 Give **one** criticism of RET. (1)

8 Name the **three** phases in Meichenbaum's Stress Inoculation Training (SIT). (3)

9 Give **one** criticism of SIT. (1)

10 What **three** techniques are used in Kobasa's programme for improving hardiness? (3)

11 What **two** explanations are offered for the beneficial effects of social support? (2)

12 What is an 'external locus of control'? (1)

Exam tip

When you are trying to decide which of two questions to answer, it is important to **check all parts of both questions** before you decide which question gives you the best chance of scoring high marks. Look especially carefully at part (c), the last part of the question. Part (c) is worth 18 marks, Parts (a) and (b) together are worth only 12.

The answers are on pages 114–15.

In all societies, people recognise and label behaviours that they consider to be **abnormal** (i.e. indicating some sort of psychological disorder). Such a label usually implies that the behaviour is **undesirable and potentially harmful and consequently requiring some type of remedy**. There are **several approaches to defining abnormality**, but no single one is broad enough to cover all instances of abnormal behaviour or narrow enough to exclude all cases of normal behaviour.

The statistical approach

● Behaviour is defined as abnormal because of its **statistical infrequency** (i.e. it is uncommon). The problem is that not all rare behaviours are abnormal and not all psychological disorders are especially rare. Statistically **rare but desirable behaviours or abilities** (e.g. very high intelligence) **are not considered abnormal and do not require treatment**.

● **Certain psychological disorders**, such as depression or anxiety, **are far from rare** in some societies. The criterion of statistical infrequency (rarity) begs the question, 'Where is the cut-off point between what is considered common and what uncommon?' A **large-scale survey in the US** (Kessler et al. 1994) found that **almost half of the respondents had suffered a psychological disorder** at some point in their lives.

Deviation from social norms

● **Social norms** are the **explicit or implicit rules** that a society has about what are acceptable behaviours, values and beliefs. Using this approach, behaviour that **deviates** from some notion of what a society considers acceptable or proper is defined as abnormal. The problem with this approach is that most people would be defined as abnormal at some time.

● Different behaviours are acceptable in different cultures and at different periods in history. **Norms change and consequently so do ideas about what is thought of as normal and abnormal.**

● Using the 'deviation from social norms' approach may result in behaviour being labelled abnormal and a psychiatric diagnosis being made because society currently finds the behaviour objectionable. The abuse of the psychiatric system in the former USSR to control political dissidents is well documented.

Failure to function adequately

● Behaviours that prevent people coping with the demands of everyday life are considered abnormal. Many people with psychological disorders (e.g. schizophrenia or anxiety) are unable to function effectively and run risks with their physical as well as their psychological health. However, many 'normal' people fail to cope with the demands of life at certain times in their lives, e.g. after bereavement or before a stressful exam.

● Failure to cope with the demands of daily living may also be the cause of mental disorders rather than the outcome. Research has shown that first-generation immigrants who may experience economic hardship, poor housing and problems in coping with a new society's expectations are more likely to be diagnosed as experiencing mental health problems.

Subjective discomfort

● Behaviour is considered abnormal if it produces extreme distress or discomfort for the person. However, most people experience extreme distress at some time in their lives. Without some other elements of abnormality being present it is unlikely that psychological suffering alone will be considered abnormal.

● Sometimes, however, people behave in a bizarre (abnormal) fashion but experience no distress (e.g. during a manic episode).

Deviation from an ideal of mental health

● Behaviour is viewed as abnormal if it deviates from the ideal of how people 'should' behave. According to Jahoda (1958), ideal mental health consists of having: a positive attitude towards oneself; the opportunity to self-actualise (achieve one's potential); the ability to resist stress; personal autonomy (not being too dependent on others); an accurate perception of reality; the ability to adapt to one's environment.

● These are such demanding criteria, however, that everyone would be considered abnormal to some extent. Ideals are judgements coloured by the beliefs of those who construct them.

Rosenhan and Seligman's elements of abnormality

● Rosenhan and Seligman (1989) identified seven characteristics of behaviour, which they thought people considered when they were judging whether or not behaviour was abnormal. The more characteristics observed, the more likely that a behaviour would be viewed as abnormal:
  ■ Behaviour caused suffering to the actor;
  ■ Behaviour was maladaptive for the actor and for others;
  ■ Behaviour appeared irrational and incomprehensible;
  ■ Behaviour was unpredictable and seemed out of control;
  ■ Behaviour was unconventional;
  ■ Behaviour caused observers discomfort;
  ■ Behaviour violated moral and ideal standards.

In conclusion

● Cultural relativism is increasingly recognised as important in discussions about abnormality. It refers to the view that 'judgements of normality and abnormality depend on the cultural experiences and biases of the person doing the judging' (Cardwell 2000).

● In other words, abnormality means different things in different cultural contexts. As geographical and historical contexts change, so do decisions regarding what is normal or abnormal behaviour.

VIV BOUND
(PERSONAL PROPERTY)

Defining abnormality

1 Describe the statistical approach to abnormality. (1)

2 What name is given to the approach that defines abnormality as 'behaviour that differs from what society deems to be normal'? (1)

3 Give **two** criticisms of the 'failure to function adequately' approach to abnormality. (2)

4 Explain what is meant by 'abnormality as subjective discomfort'. (1)

5 According to Jahoda, what comprises ideal mental health? (6)

6 Give **one** criticism of defining abnormality as a 'deviation from ideal mental health'. (1)

7 Name Rosenhan and Seligman's **seven** characteristics of behaviour that lead people to consider the behaviour to be abnormal. (7)

8 Explain the concept of 'cultural relativism' as it applies to definitions of abnormality. (1)

Exam tip

Part (c) of all questions (except for Research methods) requires both AO1 and AO2 components. The format of the questions includes phrases such as:

"Give a brief account of and evaluate . . . ."

"To what extent does research support the view . . . ."

"Consider the view that . . . ."

In all cases, 6 marks are awarded for AO1 content and 12 marks for AO2 content.

The answers are on page 115.

Numerous models (theories) have been proposed to explain psychological disorders (abnormality). Different theories make different assumptions and have their own implications for how disorders should be treated.

Biological (medical) model of psychological abnormality

Assumptions

- The causes of mental disorders are the same as the causes of physical illnesses (e.g. chemical imbalances or abnormal brain structures, caused by infections or genetic factors). Therefore, mental illness may be diagnosed, labelled and treated in the same way as physical illness.

Treatments associated with biological model

Physical interventions:

- Drug treatment (chemotherapy) – includes anti-anxiety, anti-depressant, anti-psychotic and antimanic drugs.
- Electro-convulsive therapy (ECT) – involves producing a seizure by passing an electric current through the brain.
- Psychosurgery – a type of brain surgery used specifically to change a person's psychological functioning.

Evaluation

- A genetic basis has been found for some mental disorders.

- The effect of infection on mental abilities was found when it was discovered that the syphilis bacterium produced a brain disease that resulted in the syndrome called 'general paresis' later in life, involving mental deterioration including delusions.

- ECT has had some success in treating depression but why it works is unclear. Its effects are temporary unless followed up with drug therapy. ECT is a controversial treatment leading to memory disturbances.

- Psychosurgery has helped some patients when all other treatments have failed.

- Drug treatment is popular and is effective for alleviating many symptoms of mental illness. However, its **side effects** (e.g. dependency) may be troublesome and symptoms often recur if chemotherapy stops.

- A diagnosis of 'mental disorder' carries a **social stigma** and, therefore, there may be some **ethical objections** to its use.

Psychodynamic model of psychological abnormality

The model involves a variety of approaches that have evolved from **Freud's psychoanalytic theory**.

Assumptions

- Psychological disorders are the result of **anxiety** produced by **unconscious motives and conflicts**. According to Freud, this happens owing to the dynamics of the three parts of the mind: the id, the ego and the superego. The **id** consists of **unconscious desires**, the **ego** of **rational and conscious thoughts**, and the **superego** houses the **conscience**. Because the id requires immediate gratification, it comes into conflict with the superego, causing anxiety. The ego strives to protect itself from anxiety by using a number of unconscious **defence mechanisms** such as repression, where unacceptable thoughts are forced out of conscious awareness. Defence mechanisms, however, do not resolve the conflicts, which eventually lead to psychological disorders.

- Traumatic events in early childhood may result in memories being **repressed** only to cause psychological disorder later in life.

Treatments associated with the psychodynamic model

The goal of treatment is to help clients use adult insight to **confront** their unconscious conflicts and motives. Techniques that have been employed to help do this include:
  - **Free association** – clients relax and say whatever comes to mind (with no fear of being censored) and the therapist interprets what is said.
  - **Dream analysis** – clients relate the manifest (apparent) content

of their dreams to the therapist who helps to interpret the latent (hidden) content.

Evaluation

● The model is **difficult to validate** using traditional scientific methods.

● Psychoanalysis (Freud's version of psychodynamic therapy) emphasises **sexual factors**, arguably at the expense of equally important **social factors**, and psychoanalytic therapy is accused of paying **too little attention** to current problems in a client's life that might be more important than experiences from early childhood. The approach helped identify, however, that early childhood traumatic experiences could contribute to psychological problems in adulthood.

● Psychodynamic treatments are **time-consuming**.

Behavioural model of psychological abnormality

Assumptions

● Maladaptive (abnormal) behaviour is **learned in much the same way as other behaviour** (through the processes of classical conditioning (CC) and operant conditioning (OC)).

● In the process of CC, a previously neutral stimulus (e.g. a spider) becomes associated with another stimulus (e.g. terrifying experience) that naturally produces a reflex response (e.g. feelings of panic). The **pairing** of the two stimuli soon results in the previously neutral stimulus eliciting the reflex response on its own.

● According to OC principles, **reinforced behaviour is likely to be repeated in similar circumstances**. Behaviour that is not reinforced is likely to die out. Consider someone suffering from agoraphobia, the disorder involving fear of public places. By avoiding public places the person's fear is reduced (a **reinforcement**) and so avoidance is likely to be repeated.

Treatments associated with the behavioural model

- If an abnormal behaviour is learned by the processes of CC or OC it can be changed using the same principles. Treatments based on CC include:
  - **Aversion therapy** – a person learns to associate a previously pleasurable behaviour (e.g. smoking) with unpleasant effects (e.g. nausea) and so is motivated to avoid (be averse to) the activity.
  - **Systematic desensitisation** – a person gradually learns a new, pleasant association to a previously feared object or situation. Systematic desensitisation is used to treat phobias.
  - Treatments based on OC include **behaviour modification techniques**. These are used to change undesirable behaviour by reinforcing appropriate, while ignoring inappropriate, behaviour. This technique may be used to treat children's disruptive or otherwise maladaptive behaviour.

Evaluation

- Behavioural therapies are **most effective** with disorders **where symptoms are behavioural and easily identified**.

- In the past, some behavioural therapies have been used as **methods of social control** rather than for their therapeutic benefits.

- Bandura developed behaviour theory further to include the concept of **modelling** (learning through observation). He demonstrated experimentally how observation plays an important part in learning. It has been suggested that **observational** (vicarious) **learning may also play a role in the development of psychological disorders**. For example, Mineka et al. (1984) showed that monkeys could develop a fear of snakes merely by watching another monkey's fearful response to a snake. Watching someone model a desired behaviour is often used as part of the treatment for a specific phobia such as fear of spiders.

- Therapies based on conditioning are sometimes **accused of ignoring underlying causes** and treating only the symptoms of a disorder. Behaviourists have responded that the symptoms **are** the disorder.

- Behavioural therapies pay little attention to **genetic factors** or to the **processes of feeling or thinking**.

Cognitive model of psychological abnormality

Assumptions

● **Irrational thoughts, expectations and attitudes** cause psychological disorders. Irrational thinking (cognitions) can take a variety of forms, e.g. magnifying difficulties faced; overgeneralising from a single event to arrive at sweeping conclusions; persistent negative thinking that devalues the person.

Treatments associated with the cognitive model

● **Change faulty ways of thinking** and the disorder will be overcome. Therapists attempt to teach clients how to **cognitively restructure** their thinking by:
  ■ **Monitoring** their negative thoughts.
  ■ Recognising the **links** between thinking, feeling and behaviour.
  ■ Examining evidence **for** and **against** negative thoughts.
  ■ Replacing negative thoughts with more **logical, reality-based thinking**.
  ■ Identifying and changing the **basic beliefs** that underlie the tendency to think irrationally.

Evaluation

● Irrational beliefs are common among people with psychological disorders and are particularly important in **anxiety disorders and depression**. However, whether distorted thinking is the **cause or the consequence** of mental disorders is less clear.

● **Genetic factors** are ignored.

● Responsibility and even 'blame' for disorders are **located entirely within the individual**. This may be ignoring **social factors** or **interpersonal experiences**.

● Cognitive therapies are **widely used**. Combined with behavioural techniques, they are very popular for managing stress and for treating family and marital problems.

Biological and psychological models of abnormality

1 Give the **two** main assumptions of the biological model of psychological disorders. (2)

2 What **three** types of treatment are used to treat psychological disorders by those who adopt a biological approach? (3)

3 Why was the discovery of what caused the syndrome 'general paresis' important to those who adopt a biological model of abnormality? (1)

4 According to the psychodynamic model of abnormality, what lies at the root of psychological disorders? (2)

5 Name **two** techniques used in psychodynamic therapy. (2)

6 Give **one** criticism of the psychodynamic model of abnormality. (1)

7 What is the main assumption of the behavioural model of abnormality? (1)

8 Name **two** therapies based on the principles of classical conditioning. (2)

9 Give **two** criticisms made of the behavioural model of abnormality. (2)

10 What is the main assumption of the cognitive model of abnormality? (1)

11 What, therefore, is the main purpose of treatments based on the cognitive model? (1)

12 Give **two** evaluations of the cognitive model of abnormality. (2)

Exam tip

If you are asked to give a description or an outline in part (a) or (b) of a question, do not waste time giving an evaluation as well. You will gain no marks for this.

The answers are on pages 115–16.

Eating disorders are **serious disruptions to healthy eating habits or appetite** (Cardwell 2000). **Anorexia nervosa** and **bulimia nervosa** are two of the most common types of eating disorder.

Anorexia nervosa (AN)

'AN is a disorder characterised by the **relentless pursuit of extreme thinness** and by an **extreme loss of weight**' (Comer 1998). Typically, AN begins when an individual who is of normal, or slightly over, weight decides to diet after a stressful event such as a separation. Over 90% of cases occur in females, though the incidence in males is increasing. In the UK about 1% of females suffer from AN and the peak age of onset is 14–18 years. In 5–15% of cases the condition is fatal (Hsu 1990). Other consequences of AN include **brittle bones, loss of concentration, constipation, depression and amenorrhoea** (see below).

Main characteristics of anorexia nervosa
- **Weight:** individual weighs less than 85% of expected body weight and refuses to eat enough food to restore normal weight.
- **Fear:** there is an intense fear of becoming fat and the individual's central goal in life is to become thin.
- **Preoccupation:** although AN literally means 'a nervous loss of appetite', the anorectic person is often hungry and thinks, talks and dreams about food.
- **Distorted body image:** anorectic people typically overestimate their body weight and size.
- **Amenorrhoea:** in females, the absence of menstruation for 3 cycles is a diagnostic indication of anorexia.

Bulimia nervosa (BN)

'BN is a disorder characterised by **frequent eating binges** that are followed by **forced vomiting or other extreme compensatory behaviours to avoid gaining weight**' (Comer 1998). Individuals suffering from the non-purging type of bulimia rely on dieting and vigorous exercise and do not induce vomiting. Between 1 and 6% of women aged between 16 and 40 years are diagnosed as bulimic and over 90% of BN sufferers are female (Bennett et al. 1991). Typically, BN begins after a period of strict dieting.

Unlike the sufferer from anorexia nervosa, the bulimic person's weight will usually remain within the normal range but it will **fluctuate** widely within it. The condition may last for many years and the consequences of repeated vomiting and purging include **damage to the kidneys, bowel muscles and tooth enamel, swollen fingers and stomach pain**. Those who suffer from BN are more likely than those with AN to realise that they have an abnormal (pathological) condition and are more anxious to please and be found attractive by others.

Main characteristics of bulimia nervosa

- **Binges:** episodes of uncontrollable eating when very large amounts of food are consumed. These episodes are followed by feelings of disgust and guilt.
- **Compensatory behaviours:** such as purging by self-induced vomiting or misuse of laxatives, fasting and excessive exercise.
- **Frequency and duration:** binge eating and compensatory behaviours to avoid weight gain occur at least twice a week for at least 3 months.
- **Self-esteem:** bulimic person's self-regard is highly dependent upon their body's weight and shape.

One disorder or two?

Although AN and BN differ in several respects, they also share many characteristics. Many bulimic individuals have previously been anorectic and felt depressed, and the **need to be perfect** along with **striving to maintain sub-optimal body weight** are characteristics of both types of disorder.

Biological explanations

- Animal research has found that **damage** to parts of the **hypothalamus** in the brain can result in the animal starving itself to death. **Malfunctioning** of the 'hunger centres' in the hypothalamus, therefore, might explain eating disorders in humans. However, no conclusive evidence yet exists and care must be taken when extrapolating findings to humans from animal studies.

● **Genetic factors:** Twin studies (e.g. Holland et al. 1984) have shown **higher concordance rates for MZ (identical) twins** compared with DZ (fraternal) twins for both bulimia and anorexia nervosa. 'Concordance' means that **both** twins in the pair have the disorder. Typically, concordance rates for MZ twins are around 50%. If genes were entirely responsible for eating disorders then concordance would be 100%. Therefore, **factors other than inherited genes** are also important in the development of eating disorders.

● **Biochemical factors: Low levels** of the neurotransmitter **serotonin** are associated with BN and antidepressant drugs that increase serotonin activity decrease binge eating. Problems in **endocrine functioning** have also been suggested to explain anorexia and amenorrhoea. However, there are **difficulties in knowing whether endocrine and serotonin levels are the cause or the consequence of eating disorders**.

Psychological explanations

Behavioural explanations

● According to **classical conditioning principles**, some people learn to **associate eating with anxiety** (about becoming fat and unattractive) and so stop eating to avoid anxiety. Weight loss is a sign that they are successfully avoiding the aversive stimulus (food). Similarly, the bingeing by those with BN causes anxiety, which is reduced in turn by vomiting.

● According to **operant conditioning principles**, people are **rewarded** with attention and praise **for being thin** and this reinforces dieting behaviour.

● AN and BN are more common in western societies where being slim is valued. Immigrants to the US were found to develop AN even when they came from societies where eating disorders were rare. **Social learning theory** explains such findings in terms of the new **role models** that influence immigrants. **Socio-cultural differences** may also explain the findings of Nasser (1980), who compared Egyptian women students attending London universities with women attending Cairo universities. 12% of those in London had an eating disorder, whereas none of those in Cairo did. However, conditioning and social learning alone cannot explain why only a minority of women develop eating disorders when most females in western countries are exposed to pressures to be slim.

The cognitive explanation

- Most people who diet in order to conform to some idealised norm do not develop an eating disorder. Therefore, it seems plausible that pressures to be slim trigger eating disorders only when they are combined with **cognitive factors** such as **distorted perceptions about body weight and shape**.

- Garner et al. (1976) found that more than half of their **anorectic** participants **overestimated their body size** compared with a control group, most of whom underestimated their body size.

- Although **bulimic** individuals are not usually overweight they also have distorted beliefs, their **desired body size being substantially smaller than their actual body size** (Cooper and Taylor 1988).

- Fairburn et al. (1999) found that **negative self-evaluation** and **striving for perfection** were high risk factors for developing eating disorders.

Psychodynamic explanations

- **Eating** is seen as a substitute for **sexual expression**, and **semi-starvation** as a way of **repressing sexual impulses**. According to some theorists, anorexia is a way of **avoiding sexual maturity**, the risk of **pregnancy** and the need to **adopt adult roles and responsibilities**.

- Evidence exists that some anorectics were sexually abused as children. This experience, it is argued, may be repressed but leads the person to wish to destroy her body later on. Anorexia is a way of achieving this goal. McLelland et al. (1991) reported that 30% of those with eating disorders had suffered abuse in childhood.

- Another psychodynamic explanation concerns the role of **gender socialisation**: females are taught to be self-critical and obedient.

Consequently, any repressed trauma (such as child abuse) will find expression in **inwardly directed self-harm** (e.g. anorexia).

- **Family systems theory** (Minuchin et al. 1978) proposes that an **enmeshed family pattern** of interaction may lead to eating disorders. In an enmeshed system, family members are too involved and concerned with each other. This system **inhibits individuality** and **encourages dependency**. During adolescence, a young person in an enmeshed family will be denied the opportunity to develop normal independence. Refusing to eat is a form of **rebellion** that nevertheless simultaneously **avoids disrupting the family** because members rally round to help the sufferer, further consolidating the enmeshed system. It is, however, difficult to decide if dysfunctional family systems **precede** the development of AN in a family or are the **consequence** of trying to cope with an anorectic person.

- Bruch (1974) proposed that **domineering parents paved the way for later eating disorders in their children**. For example, by insisting that a child eat food when the parent is hungry rather than when the child is hungry, or using food as a means of giving comfort are ways of confusing and dominating a child. Consequently, the child grows up with a **poor sense of autonomy and control** (called ego deficiencies) and with **perceptual and cognitive disturbances** (e.g. cannot interpret correctly its own body signals about hunger and satiety). Together these factors may result in an eating disorder because this is one way that the child can **exercise some control** and establish a sense of a **separate identity**. Evidence to support Bruch's argument comes from studies showing (a) when individuals with eating disorders are upset they rely heavily on the views and wishes of other people, and (b) internal hunger and emotion cues are often perceived inaccurately by those with eating disorders.

- Family relationships are considered to be important factors in eating disorders and **family therapy** is one of the main interventions used in treatment of them.

Eating disorders: critical issue

1 Define anorexia nervosa. (2)

2 Define bulimia nervosa. (2)

3 Give **two** characteristics anorexia nervosa and bulimia nervosa share. (2)

4 What concordance rate has been found in MZ twins for eating disorders? (1)

5 Low levels of which neurotransmitter have been linked to eating disorders? (1)

6 In what **two** ways does the behavioural approach explain eating disorders? (2)

7 According to social learning theory, why do immigrants to the US quickly become as likely as other members of the US population to develop eating disorders? (1)

8 How do cognitive psychologists explain eating disorders? (1)

9 Name **two** personality factors that are high risk for developing an eating disorder. (2)

10 Describe how sexual abuse in childhood has been used to explain the later development of eating disorders. (2)

11 What did Minuchin et al. mean by an 'enmeshed family pattern'? (2)

12 According to Bruch, what **two** combined sets of factors may increase a person's risk of developing an eating disorder. (2)

Exam tip

Remember the **AO2** component involves providing **informed commentary**, including **analysing**, **evaluating** and **effectively using** your material. AO2 is not just more description.

The answers are on pages 116–17.

Conformity

Social influence is the process by which one's behaviour, beliefs or attitudes are changed by the presence or actions of other people. One outcome of majority social influence is conformity, where real or imagined group pressure results in someone changing his or her behaviour or beliefs. Kelman (1958) identified three types of conformity:

■ Compliance (publicly conforming while not changing one's private views).

■ Identification (public and private change of view but only as long as one's group membership continues).

■ Internalisation (true, long-lasting change of views).

Why people yield to majority influence (conform)

■ Normative social influence – because they wish to be liked by others.

■ Informational social influence – because they want to be correct in their behaviour and views.

■ Referential social influence – according to Turner (1991), group membership plays an important role in the process of conformity. People are most likely to conform to the norms of their own groups. Therefore, normative and informational social influences operate most strongly within the groups to which people belong.

Research studies of conformity

● Prior to studies of conformity, Sherif (1935) studied the process of norm formation in new groups, using the autokinetic effect (an optical illusion where a stationary spot of light in a darkened room appears to move). Individual estimates of how far the light had moved were affected by the estimates of others in the group. Eventually estimates converged and a group judgement (norm) emerged. Sherif's procedure has been criticised for being ambiguous because there was no 'correct' answer (the light did not move).

● Asch (1952) investigated the effects of majority group pressure on individuals when the correct answer to a question was obvious. Participants (Ps) compared a 'test' line with three other lines. One at a time, they said aloud which of the comparison lines was the same length as the 'test' line. In each group there was one genuine P and 6 others who were accomplices of the experimenter. On critical trials the accomplices called out the wrong answer. The real P, who answered last but one, conformed (i.e. gave the wrong answer) on 32% of the trials. 74% of Ps conformed at least once and 26% never conformed.

● **Variations of Asch's procedure** revealed that individuals were **less likely to conform if the majority was not unanimous** or consisted of only 2 people or if individuals were able to write their answers rather than call them aloud. Conformity **increases**, however, if the task is made **more difficult** or if the majority is perceived as having **high status**.

● Asch's procedure is sometimes **criticised for lacking ecological validity** (not resembling real-life situations where people face conformity pressures). Some researchers thought the **face-to-face** arrangement caused the conformity observed. Crutchfield addressed this point.

● Crutchfield (1955) arranged Ps in individual booths so that **they could not see each other**. Using line comparison tasks, **Crutchfield found 30% conformity levels** and even higher levels when the tasks were more difficult. Therefore, his findings confirmed those of Asch.

● Using Asch's procedure, Perrin and Spencer (1981) found **no conformity effects in British engineering and science students**. They suggested that historical and cultural differences explained their different findings. However, when their participants were youths on probation and the majority group members were probation officers, conformity levels were similar to those found by Asch. They concluded, therefore, that **when the costs of not yielding were high, conformity to the majority view could still be demonstrated**.

● After comparing findings from many countries, Smith and Bond (1998) have concluded that **those living in collectivist cultures** (e.g. China, Fiji, Brazil) **show higher levels of conformity than those from individualistic cultures** (e.g. Netherlands, France, UK).

● Zimbardo et al. (1973) investigated **conformity to social roles** in a prison simulation study. Male volunteers adopted the role of either guard or prisoner. The simulation was stopped after 6 days because of the guards' over-zealous behaviour and the distress of the prisoners. **Zimbardo concluded that people readily conform to social roles especially if these are strongly stereotyped.** The study has been criticised on ethical grounds but Zimbardo has defended it for the insights it provided about human behaviour.

Evaluation of Asch's conformity research

Most criticisms of Asch's studies concerned the **trivial nature of the situation** he used and his **limited sample** of Ps, who were all male students.

- Research shows that **in more realistic settings, conformity rates are higher than those found by Asch** (e.g. Aronson and O'Leary 1982).

- Some research has found women to be slightly more conformist than men. Later research, however, found that **women conformed more than men did only when the researcher was male or when the group task was especially male-orientated** (e.g. Eagly and Carli 1981). Thus, **situational** (rather than personal) **factors** are **most important in eliciting conforming behaviour**.

Minority social influence

Minorities sometimes exert social influence on majorities. Initially a majority may dismiss a minority as eccentric, but under certain circumstances small groups (or even individuals) can become influential.

Research studies on minority influence

- Moscovici et al. (1969) asked groups of 6 Ps to call aloud the colour of 36 slides. All the slides were blue but added filters varied their brightness. Two Ps were accomplices of the experimenter. In the **consistent condition**, the accomplices called the slides green on all 36 trials. In the **inconsistent condition** the two accomplices called the slides green on 24 trials and blue on 12 trials. Results revealed that:
  - When the accomplices were consistent, the genuine Ps yielded on 8% of the trials (i.e. called the slides green) and that 32% of Ps called a slide green at least once.
  - In the inconsistent condition, Ps yielded on only 1% of trials.

- Moscovici and others have identified the behavioural styles that minorities need if they are to be influential: consistent but not dogmatic (need to show some flexibility); principled (not be seen to act out of self-interest); committed (e.g. be seen to have made sacrifices); topical/relevant (advocate views in line with current social trends). It also helps if minorities are seen to be similar in age, class and gender to those whom they are trying to influence.

- Clark (1998) used a research technique called the 'Twelve Angry Men' paradigm (named after the film in which Henry Fonda played a jury member in a murder trial. Initially Fonda is in a minority of one in thinking the defendant is innocent. Gradually, however, he convinces the other 11 jurors.) In Clark's study, Ps were given a summary of the murder case and the jury's discussions about key pieces of evidence. Levels of persuasiveness and the views of the jury were manipulated. Ps were asked their views about the defendant's guilt at various stages. Ps were more persuaded when:
  - The minority (on the jury) provided persuasive arguments to counter the majority view.
  - Some of the majority members of the jury began to defect to the minority view.

Why people yield to minority social influence

- Dual process theory: minorities cause majorities to think about things and this may eventually lead to genuine conversion. Majority social influence, on the other hand, usually leads only to public compliance.

- Social impact theory: all types of social influence depend upon:
  - The strength of the influence (e.g. number of people exerting pressure)
  - The status of the influence (e.g. prestige of those trying to influence)
  - The immediacy of the influence (e.g. those trying to influence are close by)

- If a minority, therefore, is to be influential it must compensate for its lack of numbers by ensuring its members have status (e.g. expert knowledge) and convey their message directly and forcefully (e.g. face to face).

Conformity and minority influence

1 Define conformity. (1)

2 Give **two** reasons why people conform to majority influence. (2)

3 Name **three** types of conformity. (3)

4 Describe Asch's procedure. (2)

5 Give Asch's main findings. (2)

6 Under what circumstances are conformity effects reduced? (3)

7 Give **one** criticism sometimes made of Asch's procedures. (1)

8 How did the procedure used by Crutchfield differ from that used by Asch? (1)

9 Did Perrin and Spencer's results confirm or contradict those of Asch? (1)

10 What did Smith and Bond conclude from their review of conformity studies carried out in different countries? (1)

11 What is the main characteristic that a minority must possess if it is to be influential? (1)

12 According to Moscovici, what psychological effect does minority social influence produce in those who are influenced? (1)

13 Which theory states that the effectiveness of social influence depends on the strength, status and immediacy of the source of influence? (1)

Exam tip

When answering part (c) of a question, remember that even the AO1 material has to be relevant and focused on the question set. Concentrate on **findings and conclusions** from studies and **avoid getting bogged down in procedural detail** which will not earn AO1 marks. Also, don't forget that 12 (out of 18) marks are awarded for AO2 content, such as evaluation.

The answers are on pages 117–18.

Obedience is complying with a direct instruction and seldom involves a change in one's private opinions. Conformity is often the result of implicit group pressure and a person may even deny being influenced by pressures to conform. Obedience, on the other hand, occurs when an individual feels that another person has a right to issue orders. On occasions, people will even excuse their behaviour by referring to their need to obey someone in authority. Most acts of obedience are sensible, e.g. heeding a sign to keep back from a dangerous cliff edge. However, atrocities carried out by the Nazis and other malevolent regimes demonstrate people's willingness to do terrible things when ordered to do so by those in authority. The research carried out by Milgram (1974) aimed to answer the question, 'Under what circumstances do people obey?'

Milgram's research on obedience

Between 1960 and 1963 Milgram studied over 1000 participants.

Milgram's original procedure

Forty male, paid volunteers were recruited to come to Yale University ostensibly to take part in a study on memory. The participant (P) adopted the role of 'teacher' and an accomplice of the experimenter, who appeared to be another genuine participant, was the 'learner' who had to learn pairs of words. The P saw the learner strapped into a chair and electrodes fixed to his wrists to enable shocks to be administered whenever he answered incorrectly on the memory test. The P sat in a room next door to the learner and operated a shock generator. He could hear the learner but could not see him. Shocks started at 15 volts and went up in 15-volt increments to 450 volts. Of course, the accomplice received no shocks. His responses and his pleas that the procedure should stop were all pre-recorded. If the P was unwilling to go on 'giving shocks' the experimenter verbally prodded him to continue.

Milgram's main findings

- All Ps gave shocks up to at least 300 volts.
- Most Ps verbally dissented but nevertheless obeyed the experimenter.

- 65% of Ps went to the end of the generator. That is, they thought that they had administered the **full 450 volts**.

- Milgram concluded that **most people would obey orders if someone in authority issued them**.

Findings from varying the procedures

Variation	Obedience rate (those going to 450 volts)
Original experiment	65%
Original procedure, women as Ps	65%
Venue moved to seedy offices in nearby town	47.5%
Teacher and learner in same room	40%
Teacher had to force learner's hand on to the plate to receive shock	30%
Teacher given support from two other 'teachers' (accomplices) who refuse to continue	10%
Teacher paired with an assistant (accomplice) who threw the switches	92.5%
Experimenter instructs and prods teacher from another room	20.5%

- Altering **situational variables** can change levels of obedience. For example, when less closely supervised by the experimenter, the Ps obeyed less.

- A study by Rosenhan (1969), using school children as Ps, showed that when the **relative status of the experimenter to the Ps is increased**, obedience levels rose (to 80% in this case).

Evaluation of Milgram's research

Ethical issues about deception, consent and protection of Ps are dealt with on pages 84–7.

Experimental validity (realism)

- Orne and Holland (1968) accused Milgram's procedure of **lacking experimental validity** (i.e. the Ps did not believe that they were giving real shocks to the learner). They suggested that the Ps were responding to '**demand characteristics**', cues that signalled how they should behave. Milgram disputed this and referred to his film evidence that showed Ps undergoing extreme stress. Interviews with Ps at the end of the procedure suggested that Ps were **convinced that the shocks were real**.

Ecological validity (mundane realism)

The ecological validity of a study is the degree to which the findings can be **generalised beyond the context of the investigation**.

- Milgram's laboratory procedures and results have been replicated in other countries and so his **findings can undoubtedly be generalised to other laboratory situations**. Orne and Holland, however, **challenged the generalisability of his findings to real-life situations**. Three studies that have investigated this claim are dealt with next.

- Hofling et al. (1966) showed that **obedience to an authority figure could occur just as readily in real life**. They arranged for a hospital nurse to receive a phone call from an unknown doctor. He asked the nurse to administer 20mg of a drug called Astroten to a patient before he arrived. This was **twice the maximum allowable dose** and hospital regulations forbade nurses taking phone instructions from unknown doctors or giving a drug without the doctor's signed consent. Despite this, **95% (21 out of 22) of the nurses started to prepare the medication** (a harmless placebo in fact) **until they were stopped**.

- Attempts to replicate Hofling et al.'s findings have failed when nurses are allowed the opportunity to **seek advice** before administering a drug. Rank and Jacobson (1977), for example, found only 2 out of 18 nurses began to prepare the medication as requested. This suggests that **Hofling et al.'s study itself lacks ecological validity**. On the other hand, Milgram's findings have been replicated many times in a range of situations.

- Bickman (1974) noted the response of people in New York to requests made by male researchers who asked them, e.g., to pick up litter or provide money for a parking meter. Researchers were dressed in one of three ways: as a civilian (coat and tie), as a milkman or as a guard. **People were most likely to obey the researcher dressed as a guard.** This field study showed, therefore, that **visible symbols of authority increase levels of obedience.**

- Mandel (1998) has criticised the way that Milgram's findings have been used to provide an 'obedience alibi' to explain atrocities committed during the Holocaust. He has shown that atrocities were carried out even when there was no pressure to obey an authority figure.

Why do people obey?

According to Milgram, a number of factors affect levels of obedience.

- **Legitimate authority:** people respect and are likely to obey those seen to hold positions of power (see Bickman's (1974) study).

- **The agentic state:** people attribute responsibility for their actions to those in authority. The Ps, therefore, were just 'doing what they were told'.

- **Gradual commitment:** Ps started giving low-level shocks and found it difficult to know when to stop as each voltage increment was fairly small. This is comparable to the **foot-in-the-door effect** where, if one can gain compliance from a person to a seemingly harmless request, they may feel committed to go along with more serious requests.

- **Buffers:** aspects of a situation that protect people from confronting the unpleasant consequences of their actions increase obedience levels.

- **Authoritarian personality:** unlike the preceding situational factors, this is a **dispositional** (personality) explanation. An authoritarian person has rigid beliefs, is intolerant and submissive to those in authority. Milgram (1974) found that, compared to those who were low in authoritarianism, Ps who were highly authoritarian tended to give stronger shocks. However, the **main conclusion of Milgram's** findings is that situational factors are important in derailing normally decent people from the moral straight and narrow.

Resisting obedience

- As we saw in the variations to Milgram's procedure:
  - **Exposure to disobedient models** reduced levels of obedience from 65% to 10%.
  - When **buffers** are **removed** (e.g. the teacher and learner in the same room), Ps were more likely to disobey (obedience dropped to 40%).
  - When the **surroundings** for the study were **less prestigious**, there was a decline in obedience levels. This is similar to Bickman's finding – when the researchers were in civilian clothing they were less likely to be obeyed. **Uniforms and prestigious surroundings are both visible symbols of authority.**

- Kohlberg and Candee (1984) found that students who were involved in protests against an authority that they perceived to be unjust were more likely to be those using **high levels of moral reasoning**. However, other research has shown that there is **not a perfect correspondence between moral reasoning and moral actions.** 'One can reason in terms of principles and not live up to those principles' (Kohlberg 1973).

- Gamson et al. (1982) showed that **rebellion against an unjust authority is more likely where Ps are in groups** and when people have time to discuss the issues involved.

Obedience to authority

1 Define obedience. (1)
2 Where was Milgram's original study of obedience carried out? (1)
3 How many participants were in Milgram's original study? (1)
4 Where did the 'learner' accomplice sit in relation to the teacher in Milgram's original procedure? (1)
5 What level of shock was given by **all** of the participants? (1)
6 What percentage of participants gave 450 volts? (1)
7 What percentage of participants gave 450 volts when the 'teacher' was given an assistant who threw the switches? (1)
8 When Milgram tested obedience in women, what percentage went to 450 volts? (1)
9 Give **three** factors that increase the likelihood that people will obey authority. (3)
10 Explain 'experimental validity'. (1)
11 Explain 'ecological validity'. (1)
12 What were (a) the main finding, and (b) the main conclusion from Bickman's (1974) field study of the effect of uniforms on levels of obedience? (2)
13 In Hofling et al.'s study of obedience in nurses, how many nurses obeyed? (1)
14 How has the view that Milgram's findings provide an explanation for the atrocities committed during the Holocaust been criticised? (1)
15 Name **three** factors known to help people resist pressures to obey. (3)

Exam tip

When asked for a 'criticism' of a study (for example, 'Outline the findings of **one** study of majority influence and give **one** criticism of this study'), remember it is acceptable to give a 'positive' criticism (evaluation).

The answers are on pages 118–19.

Ethics is concerned with the **rules or principles used to distinguish between right and wrong**. Consequently, societies such as the British Psychological Society (BPS) and the American Psychological Association (APA) have devised **ethical guidelines and codes of conduct** in an effort to prevent unethical practices in psychological research (see pages 86–7). A major impetus for the development of these guidelines came from the **ethical issues raised by research into social influence**. Remember that ethical guidelines of the sort we have today did not exist when Asch, Milgram and Zimbardo were carrying out their research.

Ethical issues arising from social influence research

Deception

- Social psychologists face particular ethical dilemmas concerning the use of **deception** in their research. Some critics believe that participants (Ps) should **never** be deceived no matter how important the issue being researched. The **majority of psychologists**, however, **believe that some temporary deception is justifiable provided safeguards are adopted**.

- **Role-play** is sometimes used in order to avoid deceiving Ps. However, the **findings** from such studies are seldom the same as those found in investigations where Ps are unaware of the purpose of the research.

- **Concerns** that deceiving Ps might result in a **lack of willingness to participate** in future psychological research **have not been confirmed**. Most Ps report that they think minor deception is acceptable.

Informed consent

Ps who give **informed consent** will have **received as much information as possible** before they agree to take part in an investigation. Fully disclosing all aspects of a procedure to Ps, however, might invalidate some research (think of Milgram's study of obedience). Two alternatives to informed consent are:

- **Presumptive consent** – tell a large number of people about the research and ask if they would have consented to participate. If they agree, then the researcher 'assumes' that the real Ps selected from the same population would also agree.

- **Prior general consent** – people who might be used as Ps are asked if they would be willing to take part in research where they may be misled about its true purpose. Only those who agree that this is acceptable would be selected as Ps for this type of study. Ps, of course, would not know if the investigation they took part in involved misleading information or not.

Debriefing

- Thorough **debriefing** is especially important when Ps have been deceived in an investigation. **The purpose of the study and the reason for the deception will be explained and care taken to reassure Ps who may be feeling anxious or foolish**.

- Milgram, Asch and Zimbardo employed lengthy debriefing procedures to reassure their Ps. However, the use of debriefing, no matter how thorough, **does not justify unethical aspects of an investigation**.

Protection from harm

- The criticism most often levelled against Milgram's research on obedience concerns the **psychological damage that Ps might have sustained from the stressful procedures**. Milgram himself reported that his Ps often trembled, stuttered and sweated. However, there is no evidence that Milgram's Ps were emotionally damaged by their experience. He followed up his Ps during the year following his investigations. None appeared to have suffered any emotional damage.

- Zimbardo has been accused of humiliating and dehumanising his Ps. Zimbardo responded by pointing to the importance of what was being researched, his lengthy debriefing sessions and the long-term aftercare given to the Ps. That is, he argued that the benefits of his study outweighed its costs. He proposed, however, that in future research of this type there should be more vigilant surveillance.

- According to Darley (1992), evil is latent in all of us and Milgram may have **begun a process whereby innocent Ps were converted into evil people through engaging in evils acts.** Milgram's post-investigation follow-ups of Ps, however, did not indicate that they had sustained any psychological damage.

Summary of BPS ethical guidelines for research with human participants

Ethical guidelines are necessary to clarify the conditions under which psychological research is acceptable.

General: Researchers must consider the ethical implications and psychological consequences for Ps in their research. The investigation should be considered from the standpoint of all the Ps.

Consent: Whenever possible, investigators should inform Ps of the objectives of the investigation. Ps should also be informed of all aspects of the research that might be expected to influence their willingness to participate. Research with vulnerable Ps requires special safeguarding procedures. Payment should not be used to induce Ps to risk harm beyond that which they risk in normal life.

Deception: Withholding information or misleading Ps is unacceptable if Ps are likely to show unease when they are debriefed. Whenever possible, deception of Ps about the purpose and nature of the investigation should be avoided.

Debriefing: Where Ps are aware that they have taken part in an investigation they should be fully informed as to the purpose of the investigation at the end of the procedure. Ps should have the opportunity to discuss their experience of the investigation and to have any anxieties dealt with. The general aim of debriefing is to restore the Ps to the same state as when they entered the investigation.

Protection of participants: Ps should be protected from physical and mental harm during an investigation. Where personal or private experiences are involved, Ps must be protected from stress and assured that answers to personal questions need not be given.

Withdrawal from the investigation: From the onset, it should be clear to Ps that they can withdraw from the research at any time. Furthermore, they have the right to require that their personal data be destroyed.

Confidentiality: Subject to legal requirements, information about a P should be kept confidential unless otherwise agreed in advance.

Observational research: Observational studies must respect the privacy and psychological wellbeing of those observed. Unless consent has been given, people should only be observed in situations where they might expect to be observed by strangers.

Giving advice: Where evidence of physical or psychological problems come to light during an investigation, investigators should inform the P if they believe that by not doing so the P's future wellbeing may be endangered. Advice about appropriate professional help should be given where required.

Evaluation of ethical guidelines

● Guidelines are just that – **guidance** (not hard and fast rules) and they are sometimes accused of being **vague** and **difficult to apply**.

● It is difficult to weigh up the costs and benefits of a study especially before the research is conducted. Investigators may have vested interests and even after the study, it may not be easy to measure personal **distress**.

● **Different guidelines** exist in **different countries**, e.g. the guidelines of the APA are more detailed than those drawn up by the BPS. In Holland, the guidelines deal with general advice to investigators while the British guidelines are more concerned with the details of research procedures.

● Condor (1991) has criticised the BPS guidelines for **limiting** its concerns to the relationship between the investigator and the participant and for **ignoring the role of psychologists in society at large**. Others accuse psychologists of perpetuating negative stereotypes (e.g. of elderly people) in books and research papers.

● The effectiveness of ethical guidelines and codes of conduct depends upon the **rigour of the ethical committees that scrutinise research proposals**. It is important that such committees include non-psychologists within their membership.

● Enforcement of ethical standards depends upon psychologists being willing to **punish those who contravene the guidelines**. The BPS and the APA impose penalties on their members if they infringe the ethical codes. However, every year A level psychology students carry out investigations and these are not always supervised by BPS members or even psychologists. Examination bodies, of course, provide guidance for conducting psychology practicals.

● **Ethical codes are revised regularly to keep pace with social change**. This is essential as the interests of psychologists and society's views about morality change over time. The need for such revisions reminds us that **ethical codes are not dependent upon universal, unchanging truths**.

Ethical issues in psychological research

1 What is meant by the term 'ethics'? (2)

2 Give **one** reason that critics offer for not deceiving Ps. (1)

3 What is meant by informed consent? (1)

4 Name the **two** strategies used by investigators as alternatives to gaining fully informed consent from Ps. (2)

5 What is the general aim of debriefing? (1)

6 What is the major criticism levelled against Milgram's obedience studies and Zimbardo's prison simulation study? (1)

7 How did Milgram respond to this criticism? (2)

8 How does Zimbardo believe that procedures such as those used in his prison simulation study could be improved in the future? (2)

9 Name **four** other areas of ethical concern covered by the BPS guidelines (in addition to consent, deception, debriefing and protection of Ps). (4)

10 Give **two** limitations of ethical guidelines as a means of ensuring ethical research in psychology. (2)

11 Why are ethical guidelines updated regularly? (2)

Exam tip

You do not have to answer the parts of the question in the same order as they appear on the exam paper. You might benefit from beginning with part (c), which requires more planning than parts (a) and (b). It is easier to pick up the AO1 marks in parts (a) and (b) if you are running slightly late than the AO2 marks in part (c) if you are short of time. However, it is important that you manage time effectively – do not spend more 20 minutes on part (c).

The answers are on pages 119–20.

Psychological hypotheses/theories are tested using numerous research methods, including experiments, studies using correlational analysis, naturalistic observations, interviews and questionnaire surveys. The data collected in psychological research is either quantitative and/or qualitative.

- Quantitative data: information in numerical form (e.g. scores on a test)
- Qualitative data: information in non-numerical form (e.g. speech)

Experiments

Psychologists use experiments to determine cause and effect relationships. Features of a true experiment:

- The researcher manipulates one or more variables and observes how participants (those taking part in the study) respond to this manipulation. The variable that is manipulated is called the independent variable (IV). The response that is measured is called the dependent variable (DV). All other variables that might affect the DV are held constant across conditions or eliminated. These are called confounding variables if they are left uncontrolled.

- There are at least two groups of participants (Ps) in an experiment:
  - The experimental group – exposed to the manipulation of the IV.
  - The control group – not exposed to the manipulation of the IV. Responses of the control group are compared with the responses of the experimental group.

- Ps are randomly assigned to groups – that is, each P has an equal chance of being assigned to the experimental or the control group. If Ps are not randomly assigned to groups the method is called a quasi-experiment.

The great advantage of the experimental method, whether conducted inside or outside a laboratory, is that it permits us to establish cause and effect links, i.e. to say if the IV has caused the DV.

Laboratory experiments

Note that not all laboratory studies are experiments. Many **observational studies**, for example, have been carried out in laboratory settings. Psychologists have made use of laboratory experiments because of the **high levels of control** they provide.

- **Advantages:** Variables are easier to **control** than in non-laboratory settings; procedures can be easily replicated; technical equipment can be employed.

- **Weaknesses:** Artificiality of the setting (**lack of mundane realism**); greater risk of **demand characteristics** than in non-laboratory settings (demand characteristics refer to all those cues in a research setting that help Ps guess the hypothesis and so lead to adjustments in their behaviour); Ps may become apprehensive.

- **Ethics:** Ps sometimes feel **reluctant to withdraw** from the laboratory situation once they have agreed to take part.

Field experiments

Field experiments are carried out in **natural settings** (e.g. schools) in an attempt to **improve realism**. Field experiments still involve **direct control of the IV** and **allocation of Ps to groups** by the experimenter.

- **Advantages:** Behaviour studied is **more realistic** than that seen in a laboratory.

- **Weaknesses:** More difficult to control confounding variables and so **the internal validity of the field experiment may be poorer than that of the laboratory experiment** where one can be more sure that the DV was caused by manipulation of the IV; more difficult, but not impossible, to replicate study.

- **Ethics:** More difficult to obtain informed consent or to tell Ps that they have the right to withdraw.

Natural (quasi-) experiments

In natural experiments, the researcher neither directly controls the IV nor allocates Ps to conditions. The study makes use of naturally occurring differences in the IV in pre-existing groups (e.g. a study of the effects of bereavement on children's social development might compare children who have been bereaved with another group who have not been bereaved).

- Advantages: Reduced demand characteristics as Ps may be unaware that they are being investigated; way of studying effects that it would not be ethical to study in any other way.

- Weaknesses: Cannot be confident about demonstrating a cause and effect relationship between an IV and a DV.

- Ethics: Ps may resent being investigated if they have not given consent.

Investigations using correlational analysis

Correlation is a way of analysing data and not really a research method. It is used to measure the extent to which two variables are related (associated), e.g. amount of TV watched and levels of aggression displayed. For more information about correlations see pages 105–6.

- Advantages: Useful to examine relationships between variables that it would not be ethical or practicable to manipulate experimentally (e.g. stressful life events and heart disease); may act as a preliminary study prior to carrying out a later follow-up study.

- Weaknesses: Cannot establish a cause and effect relationship between the variables investigated; can only measure linear (straight-line) relationships. A curvilinear relationship between two variables (e.g. task performance and levels of arousal) will not be revealed by correlation analysis.

- Ethics: Main problem relates to the way findings are misinterpreted. Many people fail to understand that a strong association between variables does not necessarily mean there is a causal link between them also.

Naturalistic observation

Naturalistic observation involves **studying animals and people in their natural habitats**. It is useful for studying behaviour that could not be studied, for example, in a laboratory setting, e.g. interpersonal interactions on public transport and animals' foraging behaviour.

● **Advantages:** Can be used as a preliminary research tool to help formulate hypotheses for further investigation; if animals and people are unaware that they are being observed, they behave more naturally.

● **Weaknesses:** Researcher has no control over the situation and so cannot always determine what causes the observed behaviour; danger of **observer effects** interfering with behaviour if those under observation are aware of being watched; observer bias may influence what is recorded and how it is interpreted; if more than one observer is used there may be problems with **inter-observer reliability**.

● **Ethics:** If observation is covert (undisclosed) then those being observed cannot give informed consent.

Interviews

The interview is used to collect information for a number of different purposes. For example, many people may be interviewed as part of a large-scale **survey** into attitudes about television and censorship. On the other hand, the interview may also be used to gather information for an individual **case study**. In the '**clinical interview**' an initial predetermined question (or set of questions) is asked. The nature of subsequent, follow-up questions depends on the answers already given. Interviews vary as to how structured they are.

Informal	Semi-structured	Fully structured
Interviewer chooses topic but thereafter listens to whatever interviewee has to say	Use some prepared questions but opportunity exists for interviewee to add own comments – technique used for the 'clinical interview'	Ask standard set of questions in a fixed order. Answers chosen from a predetermined set (e.g. 'yes' or 'no')

- **Advantages:** Informal interviews can be revealing and allow opportunities for exploring personal issues; may produce rich qualitative data. Structured interviews have high reliability, can be replicated easily and are straightforward to analyse.

- **Weaknesses:** Problems of interpreting and analysing responses from informal interviews; possible interviewer effects affecting responses and risk of demand characteristics; social desirability bias when respondents give answers in order to create a favourable impression; may be time-consuming to administer.

- **Ethics:** Important to maintain confidentiality especially if sensitive material is recorded; potential 'power' of the interviewer should not be used to coerce interviewees into answering questions they would prefer not to answer.

Questionnaires

The questionnaire is a favourite tool in survey research, enabling lots of information to be gathered cheaply. Questionnaires can be distributed and returned in various ways (e.g. by post, handing out in the street or workplace). Questions fall into two broad categories:
- **Closed questions** – respondents answer by choosing from a set of answers determined by the researcher (e.g. 'yes' or 'no').
- **Open-ended questions** – respondents are free to answer in any way they wish.

- **Advantages:** Versatile in the way they can be used and simple to administer; data collected quickly; data from closed questions easily analysed.

- **Weaknesses:** No control over truthfulness of answers given; risk of social desirability bias; poorly constructed questions may be imprecise, ambiguous or 'leading'; researcher bias may influence the way answers to open-ended questions are interpreted.

- **Ethics:** Need to take care that respondents consent to their data being used and ensure the confidentiality of information gathered.

Quantitative and qualitative research methods

1 What are (a) quantitative data, and (b) qualitative data? (2)

2 In the experimental method what is:

(a) the independent variable (IV)? (1)

(b) the dependent variable (DV)? (1)

3 What is the name for other variables that may affect the DV if they are not controlled? (1)

4 What is the function of a control group in an experiment? (1)

5 What is the single greatest advantage of the experimental method? (1)

6 Give **one** advantage and **one** weakness of laboratory experiments. (2)

7 Who manipulates the IV in field experiments? (1)

8 Give **one** advantage of using a natural experiment. (1)

9 What is the major weakness of the natural experiment? (1)

10 When is correlation analysis used? (1)

11 In what way are correlational findings often misinterpreted? (1)

12 Give **one** ethical concern raised by using naturalistic observation. (1)

13 Give **one** advantage of using naturalistic observation. (1)

14 What is a 'clinical interview'? (2)

15 What is meant by a 'closed question' in a questionnaire? (1)

16 Give **one** weakness of questionnaire surveys. (1)

Exam tip

If a research methods question requires it, make sure that you answer the question **within the context** of the study given.

The answers are on pages 120–21.

- The **general investigative purpose** of a psychology study (why the researcher has decided to conduct an investigation) is called its **'aim'**.

- A research **hypothesis** is a **testable, predictive statement that proposes a relationship between two variables**. In **experimental research**, the relationship proposed is a **cause and effect link** between the independent variable (IV) and the dependent variable (DV). The hypothesis 'Using visual imagery will improve how well words are recalled' proposes a causal link between the use of imagery and recalling words successfully. A research hypothesis is called an **alternative hypothesis** (not all research is experimental). An alternative hypothesis is either:
  - **Directional** (one-tailed): predicts the direction of the effect expected (e.g. 'using visual imagery will **improve** how well words are recalled'), or
  - **Non-directional** (two-tailed): predicts an effect but does not specify its direction (e.g. 'using visual imagery will **affect** how well words are recalled').

- The **null hypothesis** predicts that the results of the study are due to chance. In the case of an experimental investigation, the null hypothesis predicts that the IV will not affect the DV as stated in the alternative hypothesis (e.g. 'using visual imagery **will not affect** how well words are recalled').

Designing experimental research

Independent groups design

- **Each participant (P) is involved in only one condition** of the experiment; the P is selected randomly for **either** the experimental **or** the control condition.
  - **Advantages:** Can be used in wide range of situations; fairly easy to run; no order effects from Ps becoming skilled, bored or fatigued.
  - **Disadvantages:** Individual differences between groups may distort findings (random allocation to conditions helps reduce this risk); requires fairly large sample size because each P is used only once.

Repeated measures design

- Each P is involved in all conditions; e.g. the same Ps are used in both the experimental and the control groups.
  - **Advantages:** Economical in use of Ps; no risk of participant variables confounding the findings as same Ps used in each condition.
  - **Disadvantages:** Demand characteristics – Ps have more opportunity to guess the purpose of the study; order effects – Ps' performance in the second condition (B) may be affected by their performance in the first condition (A), owing to practice or boredom or fatigue. Problem of order effects may be overcome by using counterbalancing – half the Ps perform first in condition A and half perform first in condition B.

Matched participants design

- Each P in the experimental condition is matched on relevant variables (e.g. age, intelligence) with a P in the control condition. Once Ps are 'paired up', members of the pairs are randomly allocated to conditions.
  - **Advantages:** No order effects; much reduced risk of individual differences between Ps confounding the findings.
  - **Disadvantages:** Matching pairs of Ps is time-consuming and expensive, requiring a large number of Ps to begin with; difficult to ensure adequate matching of the pairs.

Designing naturalistic observations

Observers usually sample the behaviour to be recorded and interpreted. Ways of doing this include:
- **Time interval sampling** – observe and record what happens only during a specified time, such as for the first 15 minutes of each hour.
- **Event sampling** – observe and record only the events of interest, such as every instance of aggressive behaviour.

Designing questionnaire surveys and interviews

Issues that need to be resolved when designing these studies include:

- Type of questions (e.g. open or closed) (see page 93).
- Clarity in wording to avoid unnecessary jargon or ambiguity.
- Avoiding 'leading' questions.

Factors associated with research design

Numerous factors need to be considered if a study is to be well designed.

- **Procedures and instructions should be standardised.** For example, all Ps in the same condition in an experiment should receive exactly the same instructions.

- Potentially **confounding variables** should be held constant across experimental conditions or eliminated.

- **Variables** should be **operationalised**, i.e. defined in terms of the exact steps (operations) taken to measure them. For example, 'the number of word recalled immediately after learning' could be used as a measure (operational definition) of short-term memory.

- A **pilot study** should be conducted – a small-scale run-through of the investigation that is useful to identify possible problems with the design or procedures such as the instructions given to the Ps.

- **Ethical issues** – these are discussed on pages 84–7.

Assessing and improving reliability and validity

Reliability

Reliability is another term for **consistency**. It is measured by correlating sets of observations or scores. Correlation coefficients are used to indicate levels of reliability. A **correlation coefficient** is a **numerical index that represents the extent of the relationship between two variables** (see page 106).

- **Inter-observer reliability** is the **amount of agreement** (consistency) **between two or more observers who observe the**

same event simultaneously. Researchers record their own observations independently and then compare them. Reliability can be **improved** by: **training the observers thoroughly** before observations start; **agreeing how concepts are to be operationalised** (e.g. deciding exactly what constitutes 'aggressive behaviour').

- **Test reliability** refers to the consistency of people's test scores. It can be measured in several ways:
  - **Test-re-test reliability** tests for reliability over time. The same individual takes the test on two different occasions and scores are compared using correlation analysis. **A significant positive correlation indicates reliability**.
  - **Split-half reliability** – items on the test are split into two balanced halves. An individual's performance on each half should be similar if the test is reliable.
  - **Alternate-form reliability** – two similar tests are taken. If there is agreement between results on two tests then reliability is high.

- Test reliability may be **improved** by: **standardising** the testing procedures; **revising/replacing** problem test items.

Validity

There are two types of research validity:
- **Internal validity:** the effects observed are genuine.
- **External validity:** the effects can be generalised to different situations (ecological validity) and to different groups of people (population validity).

- **Problems with internal validity** may be caused by confounding variables, demand characteristics and investigator effects.

- **Problems with external validity** tend only to emerge when others try to rerun the investigation in different situations.

Selection of participants

- The participants selected for a psychology investigation are called the **sample**. The **population** from which the sample is drawn is the group of people to whom any significant findings will be generalised. Therefore, researchers always aim to select a sample that is truly **representative** of its population. There is no golden rule as to what **size** a sample should be but the **smaller the sample the more likely that it is biased**. However, **large samples** are **expensive** and **time-consuming** to use.

Psychologists use various techniques to select samples. These include:

- **Random sampling – every individual in the population has an equal chance of being selected**. Random sampling can be done by using the 'names in a hat' technique if the population is fairly small or by having a computer generate random numbers. Note, however, random sampling: does **not** guarantee a representative sample; is often **difficult** and **expensive** to obtain and so is seldom used.

- **Stratified sampling** – selecting a sample to reflect the key features of the population, e.g. a sample of 50% males and 50% females to reflect the percentages found in the population of interest. Stratified samples are sometimes **time-consuming** to select, but more likely to be **representative** of the population.

- **Opportunity sampling** – using people who are available.
  - Will not be a representative sample of any meaningful population.
  - May create problems with generalising findings.

Relationship between researchers and participants

Some problems that may arise include:

- **Demand characteristics** – cues in the research setting that lead Ps to modify their behaviour in an effort to help (or hinder) the researchers. The **single-blind procedure** where participants in an experiment do not know in which condition they have been placed can reduce demand characteristics.

- **Investigator effects** – may on rare occasions be caused intentionally if an investigator deliberately fakes results. More often the effects are accidental, caused, for example, by unintentional prompts or gestures. The **double-blind procedure** where neither the participant nor the investigator knows the hypothesis being tested can reduce investigator effects.

Research design and implementation

1 Write the null hypothesis to accompany this alternative hypothesis: 'Eating cheese before going to bed causes people to experience dreams'. (1)

2 Is the following hypothesis directional (one-tailed) or non-directional (two-tailed): 'Leading questions will affect the accuracy of memory'? (1)

3 Give **one** advantage and **one** disadvantage of the independent groups design in experimental research. (2)

4 What is a repeated measures design? (1)

5 Give **one** advantage and **one** disadvantage of a matched participants design. (2)

6 Name **two** ways that behaviour may be sampled for investigation in an observation study. (2)

7 What is a pilot study and what is its purpose? (2)

8 Name **two** ways in which the reliability of a test may be assessed. (2)

9 What does it mean if research findings are 'externally valid'? (2)

10 Why do researchers try to select representative samples of participants? (1)

11 Give **one** reason why random samples are seldom used in psychological research. (1)

12 What is a double-blind procedure and why is it used? (3)

Exam tip

The AS Psychology exam awards up to 2 marks in each unit paper for your skills in written communication. To gain the 2 marks you must express your ideas accurately and clearly and use a broad range of specialist terms.

The answers are on page 121.

Analysing qualitative data

Qualitative data – non-numerical information – may take the form of:
- **Answers** to open-ended questions.
- **Tapes** of unstructured interviews.
- **Diary accounts** used in case studies.
- **Records** made during observations.

- To analyse and report qualitative data, a researcher might use a process called **content analysis** to group together, for example, all the positive statements by a participant (P) during an interview. These statements might then be compared with all the negative comments, by considering, for instance, the **number and variety of statements made in each category**. This process can be the first step in converting qualitative into quantitative data.

- Some researchers, however, prefer to retain the qualitative nature of the data in their reports. They may concentrate, for example, on **finding patterns or theories** that emerge from what Ps have said rather than on imposing their own preconceived categories.

Evaluation of qualitative analysis

- May provide a **more rounded picture** of the Ps than quantitative analysis would allow.

- Permits **information about the context** in which observations, for example, were made.

- Allows research into that which **cannot be quantified**, e.g. how people view themselves and their relationships.

- Qualitative data may lead to **new theories and ideas for future research**.

- Researchers using unstructured interviews need to be **highly skilled** to encourage interviewees to talk freely and without fear of being judged. Otherwise, there is a risk of the **social desirability effect** when Ps try to present themselves in a favourable light.

- Findings, e.g. from unstructured interviews, may be **contaminated by the expectations of the interviewer**.

- Because qualitative findings are inevitably impressionistic they may be **unreliable** and **difficult to replicate**.

Quantitative analysis: descriptive statistics

Quantitative data is **information in numerical form**. We may want to summarise quantitative data in order to present them concisely and clearly. The techniques for summarising sets of quantitative data are called **descriptive statistics**. Two commonly used descriptive statistics are:

- Measures of **central tendency** – measures of the typical (average) value in a set of data.
- Measures of **dispersion** – measures of how much data spreads out (varies) from the average value.

Measures of central tendency

(Note that the **mode**, **median** and **mean** are **all** averages.)

The mode

- The **mode** is the **most frequently occurring value** in a set of data. For example, in the following set of numbers the number 7 is the mode: 1 2 6 7 7 7 9 11 11 14.

- When there are **two modes** in a set of numbers (e.g. 3 4 4 4 5 6 7 7 8 8 8 12) the numbers are described as **bimodal**.

- The mode is the measure of central tendency used for **nominal data** (that is, data measured in categories). For example, consider the number of students in a class who gain these different A level grades:

Grades	A	B	C	D	E
Number of students	7	11	5	10	8

The mode is the grade category gained by most students, i.e. grade B.

- The mode has the **advantage of being easy to find** and it is not affected by a few extreme values. However, the **disadvantages** of the mode are:
  - it is **unreliable with small sets of data** as a few small changes in the data set can alter the mode. For instance in the example above, if only 2 more students had gained a grade D (rather than a grade E) the mode would have been grade D, not B!
  - it **lacks sensitivity** as it often ignores most values in a set of data.

The median

- The **median** is the **middle value** in a set of numbers that has been rank ordered. For example, in the following set the median is 13: 3 6 9 10 13 22 28 31 33

- Where there is an even number of values, the median is the **average** of the two central values. For example, in the following set of numbers the median is $\frac{10+12}{2} = 11$:   5 6 8 10 12 14 17 22

- The median is used with **ordinal data** (that is, data that can be rank ordered from the lowest to the highest).

- The **advantage** of using the median as a measure of central tendency is that it is **fairly easy to find** and it is **unaffected** by a few extreme values. However, the **disadvantages** of the median are:
  - it **lacks sensitivity** as it ignores most values in a data set
  - it may be **unreliable with small sets of data**
  - it may not even be a value that appears in the data set

The mean

- The **mean** is the **arithmetic average** of a set of data. It is calculated by adding up all the scores and then dividing the total by the number of scores. For example, consider the following test scores for a group of children: 6 8 8 9 10 10. The total of the scores = 51. The number of children = 6. Therefore the mean = $\frac{51}{6}$ = 8.5.

- The mean is used with **interval scale data** (that is, data using a scale with fixed units where all adjacent points on a scale are an equal distance apart. For example, the difference between 4 and 5 metres is the same as the difference between 14 and 15 metres).

- The main **advantage** of the mean is that it uses **all** the data available and so it is a **sensitive** measure of central tendency. However its **disadvantage** is that a few **extreme values can radically affect the mean**. Calculate the mean for the following set of scores: 18 20 20 22 70. The mean is 30 and is not particularly representative of any of the scores in the data set.

Measures of dispersion

The range

- The **range** is calculated by subtracting the lowest from the highest value in a set of data and, in the case of whole numbers, adding one. For example, given the data set: 4 6 8 10 12 14, the range = 14 − 4 + 1 = 11. If data are recorded to one decimal place then the range is the difference between the highest and lowest value + 0.1. If data are recorded to two decimal places the range is the difference between the highest and lowest values + 0.01, and so on.

- The range can be used with values that are on an **ordinal** or **interval** scale of measurement.

- An **advantage** of the range is that it is easy to calculate. However, a **disadvantage** of the range is that it provides **no information about the spread of values within the range**.

The standard deviation (SD)

- The **SD** uses interval scale data and provides a measure of **how scores are spread around the mean** in a set of data. (You do not need to know how to calculate the SD for AS psychology.)

- **Advantage** of the SD – a **powerful and sensitive measure** of dispersion using all the scores in a data set. A large SD indicates that scores are widely distributed around the mean. A small SD indicates that scores are narrowly (closely) grouped around the mean.

- Where scores are normally distributed (i.e. they form a symmetrical, bell-shaped curve as shown) we know what percentage of scores lies between plus or minus 1 SD of the mean, 2 SDs of the mean, and so on.

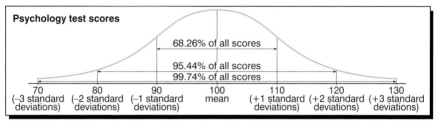

Psychology test scores

68.26% of all scores
95.44% of all scores
99.74% of all scores

70	80	90	100	110	120	130
(–3 standard deviations)	(–2 standard deviations)	(–1 standard deviations)	mean	(+1 standard deviations)	(+2 standard deviations)	(+3 standard deviations)

- The main **disadvantage** of the SD is that it is more difficult to calculate than the range.

Correlations

- **Correlation analysis** is used to measure the extent to which two variables are related. If high values on one variable are associated with high values on another variable, this is known as a **positive correlation**. If high values on one variable are associated with low values on another variable, this is known as a **negative correlation**.

Scattergraphs

- One way of displaying a correlational relationship is the scattergraph (scattergram) – see diagrams below.
  - If there is a **positive correlation** the crosses form a pattern from bottom left to top right.
  - If there is a **negative correlation** the crosses form a pattern from top left to bottom right.
  - If there is **no correlation** between the two variables, then the crosses will form a fairly random pattern.

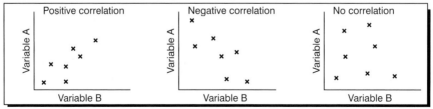

Positive correlation	Negative correlation	No correlation
Variable A / Variable B	Variable A / Variable B	Variable A / Variable B

Correlation coefficients

The scattergraph gives a fairly rough idea of how two variables are associated. To be more precise, one needs to calculate a **correlation coefficient**. (You do not need to know how to do this calculation for AS psychology.)

● The closer a calculated correlation coefficient is to + 1, the stronger the **positive correlation** is between the two variables.

● The closer the calculated correlation coefficient is to − 1, the stronger the **negative correlation** is between the two variables.

● If there is **little or no relationship** between the two variables, the calculated correlation coefficient will be close to 0.

Graphs and charts

In addition to scattergraphs used to depict the relationships between two variables, psychologists use other graphs and charts to summarise and display data.

Bar charts

● **Bar charts** are used to show the **frequencies of a non-continuous variable**, e.g. favourite holiday destinations among 25-year-olds (see below). The columns in a bar chart are separated to show that the categories are discontinuous.

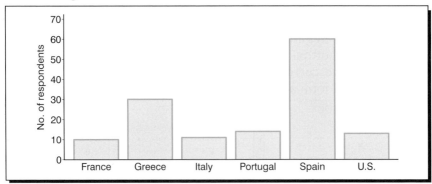

Histograms and frequency polygons

● A **histogram** (see below) displays the **distribution of a whole, continuous data set** (i.e. how frequently values occur). Histograms are a special kind of bar chart. The key points about histograms are:
  ■ Columns represent frequencies.
  ■ The whole data set is shown (including empty spaces).
  ■ Columns are the same width for the same category interval.
  ■ No spaces between columns.

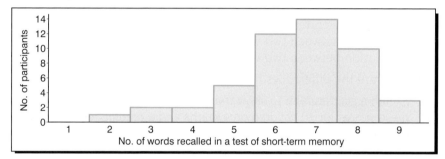

● A **frequency polygon** is used as an **alternative to a histogram**, e.g. if we wish to compare two frequency distributions. Drawing a line to link the **midpoints** of the columns in a histogram produces a frequency polygon (see figure below).

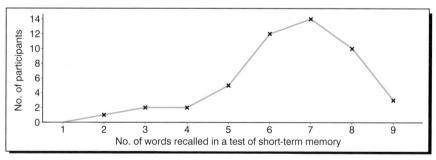

Data analysis

1 Give **two** advantages and **two** difficulties of using qualitative data. (4)

2 Name and describe **three** measures of central tendency. (6)

3 Calculate the range for the following set of numbers:

3 6 9 12 2 37 (1)

4 Give **one** disadvantage of using the range as a measure of dispersion. (1)

5 Name **one** other measure of dispersion. (1)

6 What are the correlation coefficients of (a) a perfect positive correlation between two variables, and (b) a perfect negative correlation between two variables? (2)

7 What are the differences between a histogram and a bar chart? (2)

8 Sketch a scattergraph to show the relationship (correlation) between these scores for 10 children on a maths and a reading test (1)

	Maths scores	Reading scores
Child 1	70	90
2	65	80
3	60	75
4	60	70
5	55	75
6	55	65
7	50	60
8	50	70
9	45	50
10	40	50

9 What type of correlation (positive or negative) is indicated by the scattergraph? What conclusion, therefore, do you draw about the relationship between children's reading and maths scores? (2)

Exam tip

Know what is in the AS specification. **Look** at old exam papers and **practise** the skills on which you will be assessed!

The answers are on page 122.

Check yourself answers

1   Encoding; (1) storage; (1) retrieval. (1)
2   Seven (plus or minus two). (1) STM capacity has also been measured in terms of time. We retain in STM what we can pronounce in approximately 1.5 seconds.
3   Acoustic coding. (1)
4   The students were asked to put names to the photographs of their old classmates. (1) Results – 90% of the photographs were correctly named. (1)
5   Placing information into memory after analysing its meaning. (1)
6   Information passes from one storage system to the next in a fixed order. (1) SM, STM and LTM are permanent structures of the memory system. (1) Rehearsal is used to maintain information in STM and to transfer it to LTM. (1)
7   Clinical case studies of people with brain damage (1) and laboratory experiments. (1) Note, however, that both types of evidence can be criticised. There are problems in generalising from case studies and laboratory studies are often accused of lacking ecological validity.
8   The central executive; (1) the visuo-spatial scratchpad; (1) the phonological loop. (1)
9   The articulatory loop enables us to retain information about word order and to repeat (rehearse) the material subvocally to help us work out its meaning. (1)
10   The function of the central executive is not well-understood. (1)
11   Depth (level) of processing determines if something is remembered. The more deeply material is processed the better it is remembered. (1)
12   There is no way of defining 'depth of processing' that is independent of how well material is retained in memory. (1)

FORGETTING (page 12)

1   Lack of availability. (1)
2   Owing to the passage of time (1) and lack of rehearsal (1) the memory trace is lost.
3   The serial probe technique. (1)
4   Retroactive interference: when new information interferes with retrieving old memories. (1)
    Proactive interference: when old information interferes with remembering new information. (1)
5   Failure to retrieve a memory because there are not sufficient cues/prompts to access the memory. (1)
6   It is encoded at the same time as the memory to be retrieved (1) or it closely resembles the information one wants to remember. (1)
7   Practising in a similar context might help provide cues that will aid memory in the real exam. (1) Smith (1979) found that students who learned lists of words in a basement room recalled them significantly better if they were tested in the same room a day later than if tested in a different room on a higher floor.

Check yourself answers

8 Repression. (1)
9 There may be a lack of corroborative (confirming) evidence. (1)
10 Vivid, (1) detailed, (1) long-lasting (1) memory of an emotional, (1) highly significant (1) and often unexpected (1) event.
11 Neisser (1982); (1) he thinks that so-called flashbulb memories persist because they are recounted often. (1)

EYEWITNESS TESTIMONY: CRITICAL ISSUE   (page 18)

1 When events or information are remembered they are interpreted and reorganised. (1) A person's schemas (stores of relevant knowledge) will affect how information is interpreted and reconstructed. (1)
2 **Two** from: we ignore information that is not compatible with our existing schemas; we remember only the gist of events; schema-based knowledge is used to interpret information and to fill in gaps in memory; may distort memory; help us guess what we cannot remember. (2)
3 **One** from: too much emphasis on inaccuracy of memory; does not explain how schemas are acquired in the first place; seldom any direct evidence that participants actually possess the schemas assumed to lead to their inaccurate memories. (1)
4 Participants watched film of a car accident. Some participants were asked how fast the car was travelling when it 'hit' the other car. Others were asked how fast the car was going when it 'smashed' into the other car. (1) Those who heard the word 'smashed' estimated the car's speed as 40mph, (1) whereas those who heard the word 'hit' estimated the speed as 34mph. (1)
5 When the leading question or post-event information is obviously incorrect. (1) Loftus (1979) showed that participants were able to resist incorrect information (even when it came from a prestigious source) if it concerned noticeable and important aspects of the situation. The original correct memory for events remained intact. The eyewitness participants, however, more readily accepted incorrect information about peripheral details.
6 Artificiality of procedures; (1) the explanation that misleading post-event information replaces the original memory is challenged by those who believe the new information only obscures the old. (1)
7 (a) Pen – 49%; (b) Knife – 33%. (2)
8 Those participants who saw the blood-covered knife became anxious and concentrated on the frightening 'weapon' and so did not notice the man's appearance. (1)
9 **Four** from: time spent observing event; being close to event; good visibility; familiarity of person observed; novelty or relevance of event; short time between witnessing and recall. (1/2 for each)
10 Encourage eyewitnesses to recreate the context of the situation to be recalled, (1) report every detail, (1) go through events in varying orders (1) and use a variety of perspectives. (1)

Check yourself answers

1 **Two** from: seeking proximity (closeness); showing distress at separation; showing pleasure at reunion; generally orienting towards the object of attachment. (2)
2 Pre-attachment; (1) attachment-in-the-making; (1) clear-cut attachment; (1) multiple attachments. (1)
3 The development of object permanence. (1)
4 **One** from: the observation method is prone to bias (e.g. because the observer may be influenced by own expectations and preconceptions); mothers were asked to keep records about their babies (e.g. when they showed separation protest) and such data may be unreliable (e.g. if mothers forgot incidents or faked records or completed them some time after the events). (1)
5 Type A – avoidant insecure; (1) Type B – secure; (1) Type C – resistant/ambivalent insecure. (1)
6 Some infants will have received more sensitive caring than others have. (1) Children possess different innate temperaments. Those who are innately predisposed to become stressed may be more likely to develop resistant insecure attachment. (1)
7 Since some children respond differently to the SS depending on which parent is present, it may be that the SS measures the quality of the relationship between child and parent rather than the characteristic attachment style of the child. (1) The SS can also be criticised for its artificial laboratory setting. Furthermore, we must be careful not to assume that a type of attachment shown in the SS causes a later behaviour. The findings are correlational and demonstrate relationships, not causal links, between variables.
8 Israel (1/2) and Japan. (1/2)
9 Classical (1/2) and operant (1/2) conditioning.
10 **One** from: infants sometimes form attachments to people who do not feed them; the explanation is too reductionist. (1)
11 The period between 7 months and 2 and a half years when Bowlby believed it was vital that a child develop its first attachment if it was to develop normally thereafter. (1)
12 The innate tendency (1) in infants to form a strong, qualitatively unique attachment to one (1) caregiver, usually the mother.

1 The loss of something such as the loss of the love of a primary attachment figure. (1)
2 The lack (as opposed to the loss) of something such as no attachment ever having been formed. (1)
3 Protest (1) – intense time when child cries a lot. (1) Despair (1) – child cries less and is apathetic and uninterested. (1) Detachment (1) – child is less

distressed, seems to be coping but is indifferent to mother when she returns. (1)

4 Bond (attachment) disruption. (1)

5 The mother–infant attachment should not be broken in the first few years or there may be serious and permanent damage to the child's development. (1) The term 'maternal' refers to 'mothering'. The natural mother or a mother substitute may carry this out.

6 32%. (1)

7 86%. (1)

8 According to Bowlby et al., because they were visited weekly by their parents (1) and so avoided bond disruption. (1)

9 Their problems may have been caused by their disadvantaged homes since children from such backgrounds also spend more time in hospital than children from better-off homes. (1)

10 **One** from: Genie (Curtiss 1989); War orphans (Freud and Dann 1951); Czech twin boys (Koluchova 1976). (1)

11 (a) 65. (1) (b) 42. (1)

12 Early detrimental effects of institutional care can be remedied if there is an opportunity to form attachments later. (1) However, some privation effects may be long-lasting, with adopted children having more problems with those outside the adoptive families. (1)

DAY CARE: CRITICAL ISSUE (page 37)

1 The care of children by people other than the children's parents, usually outside the child's own home. (1)

2 Examples: day nurseries (1), nursery schools (1) and childminding. (1)

3 Nursery school day care had no detrimental effects on children's cognitive development. (1)

4 **Two** from: children who entered day care before the age of 1 showed best academic performance at ages 8 and 13; children who received no day care showed the worst cognitive achievement later on; children who experienced day care showed greater socio-emotional competence later than those who stayed at home. (2)

5 The children who received day care came from more affluent families. This might be why they performed better at school later. (1)

6 Childminding. (1) Research, however, reveals great variability in the quality of childminding on offer.

7 A compensatory education programme set up in the USA in the 1960s to help children from deprived backgrounds. (1) The term Headstart is nowadays used generally to refer to the many compensatory programmes that exist. As the quality of the programmes improves, so do their beneficial effects.

8 Bowlby claimed that young children needed to have an unbroken relationship with the mother figure in order to develop a secure, lasting attachment. (1) If the child was separated from the mother by day-care arrangements, the attachment might be damaged or not formed at all. (1)

9 There is no weakening of attachments in children who attend day care. (1)

10 **One** from: Shea (1981) – sociability among 3- and 4-year-olds at nursery school; Clarke-Stewart et al. (1994) – Chicago study of children at day nurseries; Andersson (1992) – Swedish study comparing children in day care with those at home. (1)

11 Children who also have insensitive mothers. (1)

12 Stability and consistency in staffing (1); well-trained staff (1); warm and responsive interactions (1); limited group size (1); adequate resources. (1)

STRESS AS A BODILY RESPONSE (page 44)

1 The bodily response that is triggered when the brain detects a stressor. (1) The response prepares the body for action and involves the ANS (1) and the endocrine system. (1)

2 The sympathetic branch (1) – activates the body for action. (1)
The parasympathetic branch (1) – calms the body and conserves energy. (1)

3 Once a stressor is detected, the hypothalamus releases CRH (corticotrophic-releasing hormone) which stimulates the anterior pituitary gland (1) to secrete ACTH which, in turn, causes the adrenal cortex to release corticosteroids. (1) The hypothalamus also activates the sympathetic branch of the ANS (1) by stimulating the adrenal medulla to release adrenaline and noradrenaline. (1) In the US these hormones are called epinephrine and norepinephrine, terms you may come across in some UK textbooks.

4 Alarm reaction; (1) resistance; (1) exhaustion. (1)

5 **One** from: based on unethical work with animals; ignores role of cognitive and emotional factors in response to stress; oversimplifies the stress response. (1)

6 **One** from: corticosteroids prevent the growth of T cells; endorphins suppress immune functioning. (1)

7 70%. (1)

8 Hostility. (1)

9 Examinations. (1)

10 By causing people to adopt unhealthy lifestyles (e.g. drinking too much) so that they put themselves at risk of illness. (1) Tension theory proposes that people drink alcohol in order to reduce their anxiety or fear. However, there is also some evidence to suggest that moderate alcohol consumption may have a positive effect on health (e.g. reducing risk of CHD).

SOURCES OF STRESS (page 50)

1 Major events (e.g. divorce) that require one to make adjustments (changes) (1) and so cause stress. (1)

2 The Social Readjustment Rating Scale which consists of 43 life events. (1) Each event has a stress rating given in life change units (LCUs). (1)

3 Death of a spouse, (1) assigned 100 LCUs. (1)

4 **Two** from: correlational data – cannot assume a causal link between stress and illness; scale values are arbitrary; no distinction between positive and negative events; scores depend on unreliable self-reports; ignores role of daily hassles in causing stress. (2)

5 The Uplifts Scale. (1)

6 Participants identify which of the hassles on the scale they have experienced in the past month (1) and rate each for its severity. (1) Severity is shown by ticking 'somewhat', 'moderately' or 'extremely' severe for each hassle identified.

7 Experiencing many daily hassles was associated with poor health. (1) This relationship was stronger than that between life events and health status. (1)

8 Giving residents personal control over some aspects of their lives improved their health and longevity. (1) When nurses rated the residents' health they reported 93% of those given a measure of control as 'improved'. However, they rated 71% of the control group as 'more debilitated'. In a follow-up study, it was found that twice as many of the control group of residents had died compared with those who had been given some control of their environment and activities.

9 The monkey who could control whether or not it received a shock became ill with gastric ulcers, whereas the powerless monkey with no control remained well. (1) Most other studies indicate that having some control over one's environment reduces stress and protects health. (1) Brady's 'executive' monkeys were exposed to long-term stress – 23 days in fact! Having control for short periods of time reduces stress.

10 When people begin to feel they are losing control. (1) 'Density' refers to the number of people who occupy a given space. 'Crowding' is the subjective term for the stress we feel when density becomes unpleasant. In addition to feeling that we cannot move freely (are losing control), crowding may be unpleasant if we experience sensory overload (Milgram 1970) – receiving more stimulation than we can deal with.

11 Being exhausted, (1) feeling inadequate (1) and losing one's sense of identity. (1)

STRESS MANAGEMENT: CRITICAL ISSUE   (page 56)

1 **One** from: barbiturates; benzodiazepines; beta-blockers. (1)

2 **One** from: side effects; treat symptoms not the causes of stress. (1)

3 **One** from: expensive and time-consuming; no more effective than using relaxation techniques alone. (1)

4 Cognitive restructuring to modify perceived demands of potentially stressful situation. (1) Improving coping skills. (1)

5 Stress is caused by irrational thinking. (1) Ellis later renamed his therapy Rational Emotive Behaviour Therapy (REBT) to take account of its behavioural element.

6 A – activating event. (1) B – beliefs. (1) C – consequences. (1)

Check yourself answers

7   One from: difficult to define/measure 'irrational beliefs'; improvements may not last long. (1)
8   Conceptualisation (or assessing the problem). (1) Skills training practice. (1) Real-life application. (1)
9   One from: expensive and time-consuming; difficult for some people to use positive self-talk. (1)
10 Focusing. (1) Reconstructing stressful situation. (1) Compensating through self-improvement. (1)
11 Buffer hypothesis – social support acts to protect one when facing stressors. (1) Direct effects hypothesis – social support benefits health and well-being whether or not one is actually experiencing stressors. (1)
    Four types of social support have been identified:
    Emotional (e.g. expressions of caring and reassurance).
    Esteem (e.g. expressions of encouragement or positive regard).
    Tangible/instrumental (e.g. practical help such as lending money).
    Informational (e.g. giving advice or suggestions).
12 A belief that one has little or no control over what happens in one's life. (1)

DEFINING PSYCHOLOGICAL ABNORMALITY   (page 60)

1   Abnormal behaviour is rare behaviour. (1)
2   'Deviation from social norms' approach. (1)
3   Many people fail to function adequately at some time in their lives (e.g. after bereavement). (1) Sometimes a failure to function or cope may be the cause rather than the outcome of mental disorder. (1)
4   Abnormal behaviour is behaviour which produces extreme distress or discomfort (psychological suffering) for the actor. (1)
5   Positive attitude to self (1); opportunity to self-actualise (1); resistance to stress (1); personal autonomy (1); accurate perception of reality (1); ability to adapt to one's environment (1).
6   One from: Ideals reflect the values of those who construct them and so are liable to change; criteria are so demanding that most people would be considered abnormal. (1)
7   Behaviour causes suffering to the actor (1); is maladaptive (1); appears irrational and incomprehensible (1); is unpredictable and seems out of control (1); is unconventional and vivid (1); causes observer discomfort (1); violates moral and ideal standards (1).
8   The concept of abnormality means different things in different cultural contexts. (1)

BIOLOGICAL AND PSYCHOLOGICAL MODELS OF ABNORMALITY (page 66)

1   Causes of psychological disorders are the same as the causes of physical illness (1) and so they can be diagnosed, labelled and treated in the same way as physical illness. (1)

2 Drug treatment (chemotherapy) (1); ECT (1); psychosurgery (1).

3 It provided evidence that psychological abnormality could be caused by a brain disease resulting from an infection. (1)

4 Anxiety (1) caused by unconscious motives and conflicts. (1)

5 Free association (1) and dream analysis. (1)

6 **One** from: difficult to validate the model using scientific methods; overemphasis on sexual factors; treatment is time-consuming but the model helped to identify the long-term effects of childhood traumas. (1)

7 Abnormal behaviours are learned just like other behaviours. (1)

8 Aversion therapy (1) and systematic desensitisation. (1)

9 **Two** from: treatments have been misused to control people; may ignore underlying causes of the disorders; pays no attention to genetic factors or to feelings or thinking processes. (2)

10 Irrational thoughts, expectations and attitudes cause psychological disorders. (1) The cognitive model was a reaction to the limitations of the behavioural model that ignored mental processes.

11 Remedy faulty ways of thinking and the disorder is overcome. (1) For example, a therapist may challenge a person's tendency always to attribute their failures to internal, stable and global factors, e.g. 'I failed the test because I am stupid (internal and stable characteristic), hopeless not just at maths but at all my subjects (global).'

12 **Two** from: irrational thinking could be the cause or the consequence of a psychological disorder; ignores genetic factors; 'blames' the individual for the problem; however, it produced widely used treatments especially when combined with behavioural techniques. (2)

EATING DISORDERS: CRITICAL ISSUE (page 72)

1 A disorder characterised by the relentless pursuit of extreme thinness and an extreme loss of weight. (2)

2 A disorder characterised by frequent eating binges (1) that are followed by forced vomiting or other extreme compensatory behaviours to avoid gaining weight. (1) Actually about one third of the calories consumed during a binge will be absorbed before vomiting begins. It is ironic also that repeated vomiting upsets the mechanism in the body that alerts us to feelings of satiety (feeling full) and so makes us more hungry and so more likely to binge!

3 **Two** from: feeling depressed; striving for 'perfection'; wanting an unhealthy (sub-optimal) body weight. (2)

4 About 50–55%. (1)

5 Serotonin. (1)

6 People learn (through classical conditioning) to associate food with anxiety (fear of becoming fat). (1) People are positively reinforced for being slim (operant conditioning). (1)

7 Because the immigrants are exposed to new role models who demonstrate that slimness is desirable. (1) A recent survey of teenage girls in Fiji has found an increase in indicators for eating disorders since TV was introduced to the island in 1995.

8 People who experience distorted perceptions and think their bodies are too big or too heavy are susceptible to eating disorders. (1) It may seem odd but anorexia has been reported in two case studies of women who were blind from birth and from 2 years old. It appears that people do not actually have to see (i.e. visually perceive) themselves in order to be at risk of anorexia.

9 Negative self-evaluation (1) and striving for perfection. (1)

10 Child sexual abuse leads to disgust with one's body and a need to repress the experience. (1) The repressed trauma combined with a desire to punish or obliterate the body manifest themselves as an eating disorder such as anorexia. (1)

11 A family whose members are over-involved and concerned with each other's welfare (1) so that individuality is stifled. (1)

12 Ego deficiencies (e.g. lack of a sense of autonomy and control) (1) and perceptual and cognitive disturbances (e.g. inability to interpret body signals accurately). (1)

CONFORMITY AND MINORITY INFLUENCE (page 77)

1 Conformity is an effect of social influence when real or imagined group pressure results in a change of behaviour or belief. (1) Zimbardo defines conformity as a 'tendency for people to adopt the behaviour, attitudes and values of other members of a reference group.' People's reference groups are those with which they identify.

2 In order to be liked and approved of by others (normative social influence) or because they want to be correct (informational social influence). (2)

3 **Compliance** – publicly conforming to views or behaviours of others but privately holding to one's own views. (1) **Identification** – both publicly and privately adopting the views of a group but only for as long as one's group membership lasts. (1) **Internalisation** – a true conversion and long-lasting change of private views to match those of the group. (1) Compliance and identification may often be the result of normative social influence, whereas internalisation may often be the result of informational social influence.

4 A group of participants is shown a card with a test-line on it. Another card shows three comparison lines. In turn, each participant calls out which of the comparison lines is the same length as the test-line. (1) There is one genuine participant who always answers next to last. Other group members are accomplices of the experimenter. On the critical trials (12 out of 18) the accomplices give the same wrong answer. The correct answer is always obvious. (1)

5 On 32% of the critical trials, participants conformed (yielded) and gave the same wrong answer as the unanimous majority (the accomplices). (1) 74% of participants conformed at least once and 26% never conformed. (1)

6 Conformity effects are reduced if the majority consists of only 2 people (drops to only 12.8%) (1), if participants can write their answers rather than call them

Check yourself answers

out loud (1), if the majority is not unanimous (1) (even if the dissenter gives the other wrong answer conformity drops to approximately 6%).

7 **One** from: using a trivial, laboratory-based situation that lacked ecological validity or for having used only male students. (1) Other studies, however, have used women and non-student participants. Most studies using the Asch procedure have provided support for his findings, including studies using women as participants (e.g. Eagly 1978).

8 Crutchfield's participants sat in individual booths so that they could not see each other. In this way he could run a number of naive participants at once. (1) Participants had a row of switches and lights in front of them. The experimenter controlled the lights and each participant saw the same display, apparently from other participants, before he or she indicated their judgement. They pressed the switch that corresponded to their judgement when their turn came.

9 Perrin and Spencer's study using students contradicted Asch's findings (0.5); their study using youths on probation confirmed Asch's results. (0.5)

10 People living in collectivist cultures show higher levels of conformity than those living in individualist cultures. (1)

11 Consistency. (1)

12 Conversion. (1)

13 Social impact theory. (1)

OBEDIENCE TO AUTHORITY (page 83)

1 Complying with a direct instruction. (1)

2 Yale University. (1)

3 40. (1)

4 In the next room. (1)

5 300 volts. (1)

6 65% .(1) Smith and Bond (1998) have summarised many obedience studies in a number of different countries. Despite a variety of procedures, overall the obedience levels are comparable to or greater than those found by Milgram. Australian students were the exception – see answer no. 8.

7 92.5%. (1)

8 65%. (1) In Milgram's study the female Ps were asked to give shocks to male learners. However, in an Australian study where female Ps were asked to administer shocks to female learners, Kilham and Mann (1974) found only 16% obedience. The same researchers found 40% obedience among male Ps asked to shock male learners.

9 **Three** from: Perceiving authority as legitimate; being gradually sucked in by going along with a small request to start and then not knowing when to stop obeying; experiencing an agentic state, i.e. attributing responsibility for their actions to the person in authority; being protected (buffered) from the consequences of their actions; having a strongly authoritarian personality. (3) Furthermore, Moriarty (1975) suggested that people might passively obey

118

authority figures because they do not want to make a fuss. They find it easier to obey than to face a confrontation.

10 A measure of whether the experimental procedures actually worked so that the researcher can be sure that the effect apparently demonstrated is real. (1)

11 A measure of the degree to which findings from a study can be generalised beyond the context of the investigation. (1)

12 (a) People were most likely to obey the researcher who was dressed as a guard compared to the researcher dressed as a civilian. (1)
(b) Visible symbols of authority increase levels of obedience. (1)

13 95% (21 out of 22). (1)

14 Many atrocities were carried out without pressure from an authority figure (Mandel 1998). (1)

15 **Three** from: a lack of visible symbols of legitimate authority; observing disobedient models; being in a group; having time to discuss; when one is not buffered from the consequences of one's actions; possessing a high level of moral reasoning. (3) Additionally, if people feel they are being asked to fulfil **blatantly unjust requests** they might react by doing the opposite, the **boomerang effect** (Nail and Van Leeuwen 1993).

ETHICAL ISSUES IN PSYCHOLOGICAL RESEARCH (page 88)

1 The rules or principles (1) used to distinguish between right and wrong. (1)

2 Ps may be less willing to participate in psychological research in the future. (1)

3 Informed consent is given when a P agrees to take part in an investigation after receiving as much information as possible about the nature and purpose of the study. (1) Epstein and Lasagna (1969), however, found that even when all available information is given to Ps they still may not really understand what is involved and so the consent they give is not truly informed.

4 Presumptive consent (1) and prior general consent. (1)

5 To restore Ps to the same state as when they entered the investigation. (1)

6 The studies are accused of endangering the Ps' psychological wellbeing by stressing and humiliating them. (1)

7 He contacted his Ps and reported that 84% were glad to have taken part. (1) None of the Ps (out of the 40 interviewed by a psychiatrist) appeared to have suffered emotional harm. (1)

8 Procedures in future should be independently monitored (1) and kept under vigilant surveillance. (1) Zimbardo has acknowledged that he was mistaken to act as 'prison superintendent' in the simulation while he was also the main researcher. He, like the guards and prisoners, became 'trapped' in his role.

9 Ps' right to withdraw from the investigation at any time (1); information about Ps should be kept confidential, subject to the requirements of the law (1); in observational research, the privacy and psychological wellbeing of the Ps should be respected (1); Ps should be informed if psychological or physical problems that might affect their future wellbeing come to light during an investigation. (1)

Check yourself answers

10 **Two** from: guidelines are accused of being vague and difficult to apply; BPS guidelines focus too much on the relationship between the investigator and the P and tend to ignore the role of the psychologist in society at large; the effectiveness of guidelines depends on how conscientiously they are applied by ethical committees; guidelines and codes of practice are not based on universal, unchanging truths – they change over time and from country to country. (2)

11 Because the interests of psychologists change so that new ethical issues arise (1) (e.g. when to maintain confidentiality in research in areas such as AIDS). Society's view about what is moral changes over time. (1)

QUANTITATIVE AND QUALITATIVE RESEARCH METHODS (page 94)

1 (a) Information in numerical form. (1)
(b) Information in non-numerical form. (1)

2 (a) IV = variable that is manipulated by the experimenter. (1)
(b) DV = variable (response) that is measured at end of procedure. (1)

3 Confounding variables. (1)

4 Responses of the control group are compared with the responses of the experimental group to see if the IV has had any effect on the DV. (1)

5 It can establish a cause and effect relationship between the independent and the dependent variable. (1)

6 Advantage – **one** from: control of variables; easy replication; use of technical equipment. (1) Weakness – **one** from: artificial setting; risk of demand characteristics; participant apprehension. (1)

7 The experimenter. (1)

8 **One** from: reduced demand characteristics; way to study effects of variables that would not otherwise be possible. (1)

9 Cannot be sure about cause and effect link between an IV and a DV. (1)

10 When we want to measure the extent to which two variables are related. (1)

11 Assume incorrectly that a strong relationship between two variables means that one variable causes the other directly. (1)

12 Those being observed may not be able to give their informed consent. (1)

13 **One** from: useful as a preliminary research tool; observed behaviour is natural if observation is covert. (1)
Can also be used to try to corroborate findings from previous survey studies. Coolican (1999) cites Sussman et al.'s (1993) natural observation study of tobacco use among older school students. Surprisingly, it was found that tobacco was offered to others infrequently and smoking alone was more common than expected.

14 A semi-structured interview. (1) Start with some pre-set questions, but later questions depend on the nature of earlier replies. (1)

15 A question that requires the respondent to answer by choosing from a pre-set range of answers. (1)
The Likert Scale provides an example of how participants may respond to

closed questions. The respondent reacts to a set of statements by selecting a (numbered) point on a dimension of responses. For example, the following is a common dimension used:

1	2	3	4	5
Strongly agree	Agree	Undecided	Disagree	Strongly disagree

16 **One** from: no control over truthfulness or thoughtfulness of answers given; social desirability effect; effect of poorly constructed questions; researcher bias effects. (1)

RESEARCH DESIGN AND IMPLEMENTATION (page 100)

1 Eating cheese before going to bed does not cause people to experience dreams. (1)

2 Non-directional. (1) The hypothesis does not specify if memory will be improved or impaired, just that it will be affected.

3 Advantage – **one** from: can be used in many situations; easy to run; avoids order effects. (1)
Disadvantage – **one** from: individual differences may distort findings; requires relatively large sample. (1)

4 An experiment where each participant is involved in all conditions. (1)

5 Advantage – **one** from: no order effects; reduces risk of individual differences confounding the findings. (1)
Disadvantage – **one** from: time-consuming and expensive; needs many participants to start with; difficult to match pairs of participants adequately. (1)

6 Time interval sampling (1) and event sampling. (1)

7 A small-scale version of a larger study run prior to the real study (1) to test out the design and procedures. (1)

8 **Two** from: test-re-test method; split-half method; alternate-form method. (2)

9 Externally valid research findings can be generalised to other situations (1) and to other groups. (1)

10 Because this enables them to generalise their findings to the population from which the representative sample was drawn. (1)

11 **One** from: they are difficult to obtain; they do not guarantee a representative sample. (1)

12 In a double-blind procedure, neither the participant nor the experimenter (who is interacting with the participant) knows the hypothesis being tested. (1) A double-blind procedure is used to reduce investigator effects (1) **and** demand characteristics. (1) Note that the double-blind procedure includes the benefits of the single-blind procedure where it is only the participants who are unaware of the hypothesis and which condition they are experiencing.

Check yourself answers

1 Advantages – **two** from: may provide a more rounded picture of the Ps; may lead to ideas for further research; permits findings to be reported that could not be quantified. (2)

Difficulties – **two** from: needs skilled handling; findings prone to researcher bias; difficult to replicate. (2)

2 Mode (1) – the most frequently occurring value in a set of data. (1)

Median (1) – the middle value in a set of numbers that have been ranked (placed in numerical order). (1)

Mean (1) – the arithmetic average, calculated by adding up all the scores and dividing the total by the number of scores. (1)

3 Range = 37 – 2 + 1 = 36 (1)

4 Gives no information about the spread of values within the range. (1)

5 The standard deviation (1)

6 (a) + 1 (1)

(b) – 1 (1)

7 A bar chart shows the frequencies of a non-continuous variable and the columns on the chart are separated. (1)

A histogram is a special type of bar chart showing the distribution of a whole, continuous data set. There are no spaces between the columns in the histogram. (1)

8

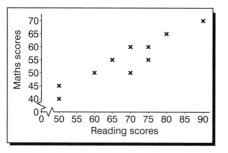

(1)

9 A positive correlation. (1) Children who have high scores in maths tend to have high scores in reading also. (1)